CAPITAL PUNISHMENT
CRUEL AND UNUSUAL?

Mei Ling Rein

INFORMATION PLUS REFERENCE SERIES
Formerly published by Information Plus, Wylie, Texas

GALE GROUP

Detroit
New York
San Francisco
London
Boston
Woodbridge, CT

CAPITAL PUNISHMENT: CRUEL AND UNUSUAL?

was produced for the Gale Group by Information Plus, Wylie, Texas

Information Plus Staff:

Mei Ling Rein, Author

Jacquelyn Quiram, Designer

Editorial: Abbey Begun, Cornelia Blair, Nancy R. Jacobs, Barbara Klier, Virginia Peterson, Mark A. Siegel

The Gale Group Staff:

Editorial: Rita Runchock, Managing Editor; John F. McCoy, Editor

Graphic Services: Randy Bassett, Image Database Supervisor; Robert Duncan, Senior Imaging Specialist

Product Design: Michelle DiMercurio, Senior Art Director; Michael Logusz, Graphic Artist

Production: NeKita McKee, Buyer; Dorothy Maki, Manufacturing Manager

CAPITAL PUNISHMENT — CRUEL AND UNUSUAL?

CHAPTER I A Continuing Conflict — A History of Capital Punishment in America 2
Colonial Period ... First Abolitionists for the Death Penalty ... Abolitionist Movement ... Decline in Abolitionist Fortunes ... Federal Death Penalty ... U.S. Military and Native Americans ... Resolving the Constitutional Issues ... Worldwide Trend

CHAPTER II Cruel and Unusual? — Supreme Court Rulings 6
"As the Statutes Are Administered" ... Proper Imposition of the Death Penalty ... Can Future Criminal Activity Be Predicted? ... Flexible Guidelines for Judges and Jurors Are Required ... Exclusion from Juries of Those Against Capital Punishment ... It Does Not Matter If "Death-Qualified" Juries Are More Likely to Convict ... Jury May Consider a Lesser Charge ... Does the Buck Stop with the Jury? ... Keeping Parole Information from the Jury ... Judge Sentencing Instead of Jury

CHAPTER III Legal Decisions — Circumstances, Right to Counsel, Evidence, and Victim Impact Statements 15
Rape and Kidnapping Do Not Warrant Death ... Mitigating Circumstances ... Not Being at the Scene of the Murder ... An "Outrageously and Wantonly Vile" Murder ... "Comparative Proportionality Review" ... When Does the Right to Counsel End? ... Federal Judges Can Delay Executions to Allow *Habeas* Reviews ... Harmless Error ... Due Process and Advance Notice of Imposing the Death Penalty ... Evidence and Appeals ... Victim Impact Statements

CHAPTER IV Legal Decisions — Youth, Insanity, Race, and Methods of Execution 29
Can a Minor Be Sentenced to Death? ... Role of Psychiatrists ... Can an Insane Person Be Executed? ... Can a Mentally Retarded Person Be Executed? ... Competency Standard ... Race as a Consideration ... Methods of Execution

CHAPTER V Death Penalty Statutes and Methods 44
Capital Offenses ... Recent Statutory Changes ... Recent Challenges to State Death Penalty Laws ... Minimum Age for Execution ... Executing Mentally Retarded Persons ... Death Penalty Methods ... Public and Private Executions

CHAPTER VI Historical Statistics 53
How Many Executions? ... Where Are the Executions? ... Gender ... Race and Ethnicity ... Crimes Committed ... Method of Execution

CHAPTER VII Under Sentence of Death 59
An Ever-Increasing Number ... Geographic Distribution ... Gender and Race ... Characteristics of Prisoners ... Criminal History of Death Row Inmates ... A Long Wait ... Getting off Death Row ... Automatic Review ... Executing the Innocent ... Fairness and the Death Penalty ... The Costs of Executions

CHAPTER VIII Public Attitudes Toward Capital Punishment 75
Support Increasing ... Acceptable Penalty for Murder ... Support for Capital Punishment Is Lower in Specific Cases ... Is the Death Penalty Imposed Too Often? ... Death Penalty Favored Even If Some Are Innocent ... Crimes Deserving the Death Penalty ... Deterrent or Not?

CHAPTER IX Capital Punishment Around the World 81
United Nations Resolutions ... Retentionist Countries ... *De Facto* Abolitionists ... Abolitionist Countries ... Death Penalty Against Minors

CHAPTER X The Debate — Capital Punishment Should Be Maintained 91

CHAPTER XI The Debate — Capital Punishment Should Be Abolished 100

IMPORTANT NAMES AND ADDRESSES 109
RESOURCES 110
INDEX 111

CHAPTER I

A CONTINUING CONFLICT —
A HISTORY OF CAPITAL PUNISHMENT IN AMERICA

THE COLONIAL PERIOD

Since the first European settlers arrived in America, the death penalty has been accepted as just punishment for a variety of offenses. The English Penal Code, which applied to the British colonies, listed 14 capital offenses, but actual practice varied from colony to colony. In the Massachusetts Bay Colony, 12 crimes warranted the death penalty — idolatry, witchcraft, blasphemy, rape, statutory rape, kidnapping, perjury in a trial involving a possible death sentence, rebellion, murder, assault in sudden anger, adultery, and buggery (sodomy). In the statute, each crime was accompanied by Old Testament quotations justifying the capital punishment. Later, arson, treason, and grand larceny were added.

In 1608, the first recorded execution in the new colonies occurred in the Jamestown colony of Virginia. Captain George Kendall, accused of spying for Spain, received the death penalty.

In contrast, the Quakers adopted much milder laws. The Royal Charter for South Jersey (1646) did not permit capital punishment for any crime, and there was no execution until 1691. In Pennsylvania, William Penn's Great Act of 1682 limited the death penalty to treason and murder. Most states, however, followed the much harsher British codes. For example, in New York, hitting one's parent was punishable by death.

THE FIRST ABOLITIONISTS
FOR THE DEATH PENALTY

Although the Founding Fathers commonly accepted the death penalty, many early Americans opposed capital punishment. In the late eighteenth century, Dr. Benjamin Rush (1745-1813), considered to be the founder of the American abolitionist movement, decried capital punishment. He attracted the support of Benjamin Franklin, and it was at Franklin's home in Philadelphia that Rush became one of the first Americans to propose a "House of Reform," a prison where criminals could be detained until they changed their anti-social behavior. Consequently, in 1790, the Walnut Street Jail, the primitive seed from which the American penal system grew, was built in Philadelphia. (See *Prisons and Jails — A Deterrent to Crime?*, Information Plus, Wylie, Texas, 1999.)

Dr. Rush published numerous pamphlets, the most notable of which was *Inquiry into the Justice and Policy of Punishing Murder by Death*. Rush argued that the biblical support given capital punishment was questionable and that the threat of hanging did not deter crime. Influenced by the philosophy of the Enlightenment (the Age of Reason in the mid- to late 1700s), Rush believed the state exceeded its granted powers when it executed a citizen. In addition to Franklin, Rush attracted many other Pennsylvanians to his cause, including Pennsylvania's Attorney General, William

Bradford. As a result, in 1794, Pennsylvania repealed the death penalty for all crimes except first-degree murder.

THE ABOLITIONIST MOVEMENT

Rush's proposals attracted many followers, and numerous petitions, with the intent to abolish all capital punishment, were presented in Ohio, New Jersey, New York, and Massachusetts. No state, however, reversed its laws.

The second quarter of the nineteenth century was a time of reform in America. Capital punishment opponents rode the tide of righteousness and indignation created by anti-saloon and anti-slavery advocates. Abolitionist societies sprang up, especially along the Atlantic Coast. In 1845, the American Society for the Abolition of Capital Punishment was founded.

In the late 1840s, Horace Greeley, the editor and founder of the *New York Tribune* and a leading advocate of most abolitionist causes, led the crusade against the death penalty. In 1846, Michigan, still a U.S. territory, was the first to abolish the death penalty for all crimes except treason. The law took effect the following year, making Michigan, for all practical purposes, the first English-speaking jurisdiction in the world to abolish the death penalty for common crimes. In 1852, Rhode Island included even treason when it outlawed hanging, as did Wisconsin a year later. Most states began limiting the number of capital crimes. In fact, outside the South, murder and treason became the only acts warranting capital punishment.

Opponents of the death penalty initially benefited from abolitionist sentiment, but as the Civil War neared, concern about the death penalty was lost amid the growing anti-slavery movement. It was not until after the Civil War that Maine and Iowa abolished the death penalty. However, almost immediately their legislatures reversed themselves and reinstated the death penalty. In 1887, Maine again reversed itself and abolished capital punishment. Colorado also abolished capital punishment

but apparently against the will of many of its citizens. At least twice, these citizens lynched convicted murderers; in response, the state restored the death penalty.

Meanwhile, the federal government, following considerable debate, reduced the number of federal crimes punishable by death to three — treason, murder, and rape. In no instance was it to be mandatory.

A DECLINE IN
ABOLITIONIST FORTUNES

At the turn of the century, death penalty abolitionists again took advantage of American reformism as the Progressives (liberal reformers) tried to correct the deficiencies of the American system. Between 1907 and 1917, six states and Puerto Rico abolished capital punishment, but the momentum did not last. By 1920, five states had reinstated it. The Prohibition Era, characterized by frequent disdain for law and order, almost destroyed the abolitionist movement as many Americans began to believe that the death penalty was the only proper punishment for gangsters who committed murder.

Only the determined efforts of the famed Clarence Darrow, the "attorney for the damned"; Lewis E. Lawes, the abolitionist warden of Sing Sing Prison (New York); and the American League to Abolish Capital Punishment (founded in 1927) prevented the movement's complete collapse. Nonetheless, of the 16 states and jurisdictions (including Puerto Rico) that outlawed capital punishment after 1845, only seven — Michigan, Rhode Island, Wisconsin, Maine, North Dakota, Minnesota, and Puerto Rico — had no major death penalty statute at the beginning of the 1950s. In fact, between 1917 and 1957, no state abolished the death penalty.

The movement made a mild comeback in the mid-1950s, and the issue was discussed in several state legislatures. However, in 1957, only the then-territories of Alaska and Hawaii abolished the death penalty. In the states, the movement's singular success in Delaware (1958) was reversed three years later (1961), a major disappointment for death penalty opponents.

The abolitionists were able to recover during the civil rights movement of the 1960s. Michigan (1963, for treason), Oregon (1964), Iowa (1965), and West Virginia (1965) all abolished capital punishment, while many other states sharply reduced the number of crimes punishable by the death penalty. Oregon and New York have since reinstated capital punishment. In 1995, New York became the thirty-eighth state to reinstate the death penalty, ending its 18-year moratorium on capital punishment. At yearend 1998, 38 states, the federal government, and the U.S. military had the death penalty (see Chapter V).

FEDERAL DEATH PENALTY

The federal government no longer lists rape as one of the crimes punishable by death, but it continues to impose the death penalty for murder, treason, and espionage. Over the years, the federal government has added to the number of federal offenses punishable by the death penalty (see Chapter V). From 1927 to 1963, the federal government executed 34 persons, including two women. The last federal execution was on February 15, 1963, when Victor Feguer was hanged in Iowa for kidnapping and murder.

In 1988, Congress enacted the Anti-Drug Abuse Act (PL 100-690), which included a drug-kingpin provision, allowing the death penalty for murder resulting from large-scale illegal drug dealing. Since its enactment, as of January 2000, six people have been sentenced to death under this provision.

In 1994, the Violent Crime Control and Law Enforcement Act (PL 103-322; also known as the Federal Death Penalty Act of 1994) added more than 50 crimes punishable by death. Among these federal crimes are murder of certain government officials, kidnapping resulting in death, murder for hire, fatal drive-by shootings, sexual abuse crimes

resulting in death, carjacking resulting in death, and some crimes not resulting in death, such as running a large-scale drug enterprise. Under the act, 15 persons have been sentenced to death, including Oklahoma City bomber Timothy J. McVeigh.

In 1996, Congress passed the Anti-Terrorism and Effective Death Penalty Act (PL 104-132), allowing for only one *habeas corpus* petition (whereby death row inmates request federal review of their convictions), which must be filed within six months from their final state court sentencing.

The 1988 Anti-Drug Abuse Act did not provide for the method of federal execution, although President George Bush authorized the use of lethal injection. According to the 1994 law, the method of execution will be the same as that used in the state where the sentencing occurs. If the state does not allow the death penalty, the judge would choose a state with the death penalty.

Federal prisoners used to be imprisoned in the state where the trial was held. It was not until the summer of 1999 that the Federal Bureau of Prisons built a 50-cell federal death house in Terre Haute, Indiana, to accommodate the condemned.

The U.S. MILITARY AND NATIVE AMERICANS

The U.S. government has let Native American reservations use their own discretion regarding the death penalty. The U.S. military has its own death penalty law, with lethal injection as the method of execution. Eight men are on the military death row, but no execution has occurred for over 30 years.

RESOLVING THE CONSTITUTIONAL ISSUES

Until the 1960s, there was legally no question that the death penalty was acceptable under the United States Constitution. Then, in 1963, Supreme Court Justice Goldberg (joined by Justices Douglas and Brennan), dissenting from a rape case in which the defendant had been sentenced to death (*Rudolph v. Alabama,* 375 U.S. 889), raised the question of the legality of the death penalty. The filing of a large number of lawsuits in the late 1960s led to an implied moratorium (temporary suspension) on carrying out the death penalty, which lasted until 1977, when the state of Utah executed a convicted murderer (see Chapter II).

Since 1972, with *Furman v. Georgia* (408 U.S. 238) and the accompanying cases, the Supreme Court has been defining and refining what is and is not acceptable under the U.S. Constitution. With the replacement of Chief Justice Earl Warren by Chief Justice Warren Burger and his later replacement by Chief Justice William Rehnquist, the Court majority has generally interpreted the death penalty as worthy of extra attention because of the seriousness of the consequences, but most assuredly as acceptable punishment for murder. There can be little question that the High Court's position reflects that of the American public. See Chapter VIII. (See also Chapters II, III, and IV for court rulings on capital punishment.)

FUTURE CONSIDERATIONS

The grounds for judicial appeal are becoming narrower. Some observers believe that the time is drawing near when all constitutional issues will have been raised and decided, and the condemned will have no more recourse to the courts, based on unresolved constitutional issues, to postpone their execution.

The 1996 Anti-Terrorism and Effective Death Penalty Act has limited the number of *habeas corpus* petitions, and some states have required strict filing deadlines and sped up the appeals process. Consequently, more inmates' lives will be in the hands of the governors and/or clemency boards. As of 1999, since the reinstatement of the death penalty, 41 death row inmates have received a commutation of their death sentences. In 1999, five death row inmates received reprieve, the most notable being that of Darrell Mease, who was scheduled for execution on February 10, 1999. On January 28, 1999, as a tribute to Pope John Paul II, who requested clemency for Mease during his visit to St. Louis, Missouri, Governor Mel Carnahan commuted Mease's sentence to life imprisonment without parole.

Opponents of capital punishment believe that the unclear language of the 1996 law (see above) has allowed for varying interpretations in federal appeals courts, which will eventually call for the Supreme Court to resolve.

WORLDWIDE TREND

The *de facto* (in practice, as different from *de jure,* in law) moratorium from 1967 to 1977 paralleled a general worldwide movement, especially among Western nations, towards the abolition of capital punishment. While the United States resumed executions during the late 1970s, most of the Western world either formally or informally abolished it.

Today, among the Western democratic nations (with which the United States traditionally compares itself), only the United States imposes the death penalty. (There are technical exceptions — Israel, for example, despite continuing conflict, maintains the death penalty for "crimes against mankind" but has executed only Adolf Eichmann. Some countries still maintain the death penalty for treason — although no Western democracy has actually imposed it.) One of the first acts of the parliaments of many of the Eastern European countries after the fall of Communism was to abolish capital punishment.

In 1999, then-President Boris Yeltsin of Russia commuted 716 death sentences to life imprisonment. As of December 18, 1999, more than half the countries in the world (106) had abolished the death penalty in law or in practice. On August 24, 1999, the United Nations Sub-Commission on the Promotion and Protection of Human Rights, in light of the coming millennium, called for a moratorium on the death penalty (see Chapter IX).

CHAPTER II

CRUEL AND UNUSUAL? — SUPREME COURT RULINGS

In 1967, a coalition of anti-death penalty groups sued Florida and California, the states with the most inmates on death row at that time. A *de facto* moratorium (temporary suspension) of inmate execution resulted, pending a Supreme Court decision on the constitutionality of the death penalty. This moratorium lasted until 1977 when Gary Gilmore, virtually at his own request, was executed by the State of Utah.

"AS THE STATUTES ARE ADMINISTERED"

On June 29, 1972, a split 5-4 Supreme Court reached the landmark decision *Furman v. Georgia* (408 U.S. 238 — that included *Jackson v. Georgia* and *Branch v. Texas*), which held that "as the statutes are administered ... the imposition and carrying out of the death penalty [constitute] cruel and unusual punishment in violation of the Eighth and Fourteenth Amendments." The justices, whether they were of the majority opinion or of the dissenting opinion, could not agree on the arguments explaining why they opposed or supported the death penalty. Justice Douglas, in his concurring majority opinion, quoted former Attorney General Ramsey Clark.

> It is the poor, the sick, the ignorant, the powerless, and the hated who are executed.... [The law] leaves to the uncontrolled discretion of judges and juries the determination whether defendants committing these crimes should die or be imprisoned.... These discretionary statutes are unconstitutional.

Justice Brennan stated,

> [A]t bottom, the Cruel and Unusual Punishments Clause prohibits the infliction of uncivilized and inhumane punishments. The State, even as it punishes, must treat its members with respect for their intrinsic worth as human beings. A punishment is "cruel and unusual," therefore, if it does not comport with human dignity....

Justice Stewart stressed another point, saying,

> These death sentences are cruel and unusual in the same way that being struck by lightning is cruel and unusual. For, of all the people convicted of rapes and murders are ... a capriciously (unpredictably) selected random handful upon whom the sentence of death has in fact been imposed....

This did not mean that Justice Stewart would rule out the death penalty. He believed that the death penalty was justified but would like to see a more equitable (fair) system of determining who should be executed. He added,

> The instinct for retribution (punishment or vengeance for a wrong or injury) is part of the nature of man, and channeling that instinct in the administration of criminal justice serves an important purpose in promoting the stability of a society governed by law. When people begin to believe that organized society is unwilling or unable to impose upon criminal offenders the pun-

ishment they "deserve," then there are sown the seeds of anarchy — of self help, vigilante justice, and lynch law.

Justice White stated that, "as it is presently administered, the penalty is so infrequently imposed that the threat of execution is too attenuated (lessened in its seriousness) to be of substantial service to criminal justice." Justice Marshall, however, concluded that "the death penalty is an excessive and unnecessary punishment which violates the Eighth Amendment.... It is morally unacceptable to the people of the United States at this time in their history."

Not Everyone Agreed

Chief Justice Warren Burger, dissenting, observed that "the constitutional prohibition against 'cruel and unusual punishments' cannot be construed to bar the imposition of the punishment of death." Justice Blackmun feared "that statutes stricken down today will be reenacted by state legislatures to prescribe the death penalty for specified crimes without any alternative for the imposition of a lesser punishment in the discretion of the judge or jury."

Justice Powell declared,

I find no support in the language of the Constitution, in its history, or in the cases arising under it — for the view that this Court may invalidate a category of penalties because we deem less severe penalties adequate to serve the ends of penology.... This Court has long held that legislative decisions in this area, which are within the special competency of that branch, are entitled to the presumption of validity. (The Court would not question the validity of a government entity properly doing its job unless its actions were way out of line.)

Justice Rehnquist concurred, adding the following comment:

How can government by the elected representatives of the people coexist with the power of the federal judiciary, whose members are constitutionally insulated from responsiveness to the popular will, ... declare invalid laws duly enacted by the popular branches of government?

Only Justices Brennan and Marshall concluded that the Eighth Amendment prohibited the death penalty for every crime and under all circumstances. Justice Douglas' opinions did not necessarily require the final abolition of the penalty. Justices Stewart and White concluded that, because of the capricious imposition of the sentence, the death penalty violated the Eighth Amendment.

Consequently, most state legislatures went to work to revise their capital punishment laws. They strove to make these laws more equitable in order to swing the votes of Stewart and White (and later that of John Stevens, who replaced the retired Justice Douglas).

PROPER IMPOSITION
OF THE DEATH PENALTY

Four years later, on July 2, 1976, the Supreme Court ruled decisively on a series of cases. In a 7-2 decision, the justices ruled that the death penalty was, indeed, constitutional as presented in some new state laws. With Brennan and Marshall dissenting, the Court stressed (just in case *Furman* had been misunderstood) that "the death penalty is not a form of punishment that may never be imposed, regardless of the circumstances of the offense, regardless of the procedure followed in reaching the decision." Furthermore, "the infliction of death as a punishment for murder is not without justification and ... is not unconstitutionally severe."

The ruling upheld death penalty statutes in Georgia (*Gregg v. Georgia,* 428 U.S. 153, the source of the above quote), Florida (*Proffitt v. Florida,* 428 U.S. 242), and Texas (*Jurek v. Texas,* 428 U.S. 262), but struck down laws in North Carolina (*Woodson v. North Carolina,* 428 U.S. 280) and Louisiana (*Roberts v. Louisiana,* 428 U.S. 40) as being too rigid in imposing capital punishment for certain crimes.

Citing the new Georgia laws in *Gregg v. Georgia,* Justice Stewart supported the bifurcated (two-part) trial system, where the accused would first be tried to determine his or her guilt. Then, in a separate trial, the jury would consider whether the convicted person deserved the death penalty or whether mitigating (lessening the gravity of the crime) circumstances warrant a lesser sentence, usually life imprisonment. This system meets the requirements demanded by *Furman.* Noting how the Georgia statutes fulfilled these demands, Justice Stewart observed,

> These procedures [established by the Georgia statutes] require the jury to consider the circumstances of the crime and the criminal before it recommends sentence. No longer can a Georgia jury do as *Furman's* jury did: reach a finding of the defendant's guilt and then, without guidance or direction, decide whether he should live or die. Instead, the jury's attention is directed to the specific "circumstances of the crime: Was it committed in the course of another capital felony? Was it committed for money? Was it committed upon a peace officer or judicial officer? Was it committed in a particularly heinous way or in a manner that endangered the lives of many persons?" In addition, the jury's attention is focused on the characteristics of the person who committed the crime: Does he have a record of prior convictions for capital offenses? Are there any special facts about this defendant that mitigate against imposing capital punishment (e.g., his youth, the extent of his cooperation with the police, his emotional state at the time of the crime)? As a result, while some jury discretion still exists, "the discretion to be exercised is controlled by clear and objective standards so as to produce non-discriminatory application."

In addition, the Georgia law required that all death sentences be automatically appealed to the state supreme court, an "important additional safeguard against arbitrariness and caprice." The two-part trial system has since been adopted in the trials of all capital murder cases.

In *Proffitt v. Florida*, the High Court upheld Florida's death penalty laws that had a bifurcated trial system similar to Georgia's. However, in Florida, the sentence was determined by the trial judge rather than by the jury, who assumed an advisory role during the sentencing phase. The Court found Florida's sentencing guidelines adequate in preventing unfair imposition of the death sentence.

CAN FUTURE CRIMINAL ACTIVITY BE PREDICTED?

In *Jurek v. Texas*, the issue centered on whether a jury can satisfactorily determine the future actions of a convicted murderer. (See Chapter IV for the role of psychiatrists in determining future actions.) The Texas statute required that during the sentencing phase of a trial, after the defendant had been found guilty, the jury would determine whether it is probable the defendant would commit future criminal acts of violence that would threaten society. While agreeing with Jurek's attorneys that predicting future behavior is not easy, Justice Stewart noted,

> The fact that such a determination is difficult, however, does not mean that it cannot be made. Indeed, prediction of future criminal conduct is an essential element in many of the decisions rendered throughout our criminal justice system. The decision whether to admit a defendant to bail, for instance, must often turn on a judge's prediction of the defendant's future conduct. Any sentencing authority must predict a convicted person's probable future conduct when it engages in the process of determining what punishment to impose. For those sentenced to prison, these same predictions must be made by parole authorities. The task that a Texas jury must

perform in answering the statutory question is thus basically no different from the task performed countless times each day throughout the American system of criminal justice.

FLEXIBLE GUIDELINES FOR JUDGES AND JURORS ARE REQUIRED

In *Woodson v. North Carolina*, the Supreme Court addressed for the first time the question of whether the jury's handing down of a death sentence pursuant to North Carolina's mandatory death penalty for all first-degree murders constituted cruel and unusual punishment within the meaning of the Eighth and Fourteenth Amendments. The justices held that North Carolina's new statute provided "no standards to guide the jury in its inevitable exercise of the power to determine which first-degree murderer shall live and which shall die." Furthermore, the North Carolina law did not let the jury consider the convicted defendant's character, criminal record, or the circumstances of the crime before the imposition of the death sentence.

The Louisiana mandatory death sentence for first-degree murder suffered from similar inadequacies. It did, however, permit the jury to consider lesser offenses such as second-degree murder. In *Roberts v. Louisiana*, the Supreme Court rejected the Louisiana law because it forced the jury to find the defendant guilty of a lesser crime in order to avoid imposing the death penalty. The jury did not have the option of first determining if the accused was indeed guilty of first-degree murder for the crime he had actually committed and then recommending a lesser sentence if there were mitigating circumstances to support it.

As a result of either *Furman* or *Gregg*, or both, virtually every state's capital punishment statute had to be rewritten. These statutes would provide flexible guidelines for judges and juries so that they might fairly decide capital cases and consider, then impose, if necessary, the death penalty.

EXCLUSION FROM JURIES OF THOSE AGAINST CAPITAL PUNISHMENT

In *Witherspoon v. Illinois* (391 U.S. 510, 1968), the Supreme Court found unconstitutional the exclusion from juries of all who opposed the death penalty without determining whether their ethical beliefs would compel them to reject capital punishment. This selective process would result in a jury that would not be representative of the community.

However, the findings in *Witherspoon* did not mean that a person against the death penalty could not be excluded. According to the justices,

[A prospective juror must] be willing to *consider* all the penalties provided by [the] state law, and ... not be irrevocably committed before the trial has begun, to vote against the penalty of death regardless of the facts and circumstances that might emerge in the course of proceedings.

[Based on] presently available knowledge, we simply cannot conclude ... that the exclusion of jurors opposed to capital punishment results in an unrepresentative jury on the issue of guilt or substantially increases the risk of conviction.

Consequently, based on *Witherspoon*, it has become the practice in most states to exclude prospective jurors who indicate that they could not possibly in good conscience return a death penalty. In *Lockett v. Ohio* (438 U.S, 586, 1978, see Chapter III) the Supreme Court upheld *Witherspoon* when it dismissed Lockett's contention that the exclusion of four prospective jurors who opposed the death penalty denied her an impartial jury.

Weakening *Witherspoon*

In *Wainwright v. Witt* (469 U.S. 412, 1985), a 7-2 Supreme Court majority eased the strict requirements of *Witherspoon*. Writing for the majority, Justice Rehnquist declared that the new capital punishment procedures left less discretion to jurors. Rehnquist indicated that potential jurors in capital cases should be excluded from jury duty in a manner similar to how they were excluded in noncapital cases.

No longer would a juror's "automatic" bias against imposing the death penalty have to be proved with "unmistakable clarity." A prosecutor could not be expected to ask all the questions necessary to determine if a juror would automatically rule against the death penalty or fail to convict a defendant if he or she were likely to face execution. Fundamentally, the question of exclusion from a jury should be determined by the interplay of the prosecutor and the defense lawyer and by the decision of the judge based on his or her initial observations of the prospective juror. Judges can see first-hand whether prospective jurors' beliefs would bias their ability to impose the death penalty.

In his dissent, Justice Brennan claimed that making it easier to eliminate those who opposed capital punishment from the jury created a jury not only more likely to impose the death sentence, but also more likely to convict. He also attacked the majority interpretation that now treated exclusion from a capital case as being similar to exclusion from any other case.

IT DOES NOT MATTER IF "DEATH-QUALIFIED" JURIES ARE MORE LIKELY TO CONVICT

In *Lockhart v. McCree* (476 U.S. 162, 1986), the Supreme Court resolved the issue of a fair trial with a "death-qualified" jury. Ardia McCree was convicted of murdering Evelyn Boughton while robbing her gift shop and service station in Camden, Arkansas. In accordance with Arkansas law, the trial judge removed eight prospective jurors because they indicated they could not, under any circumstances, vote for the imposition of the death sentence. The resulting jury then convicted McCree and, although the state sought the death penalty, sentenced McCree to life imprisonment without parole.

McCree appealed, claiming that the removal of the so-called "*Witherspoon*-excludables" violated his right to a fair trial under the Sixth and Fourteenth Amendments. These amendments guaranteed that his guilt or innocence would be determined by an impartial jury selected from a representative cross-section of the community, which would include people strongly opposed to the death penalty. Both the federal district court and the federal court of appeals agreed with McCree, but in a 6-3 decision, the Supreme Court disagreed.

The High Court majority did not accept the validity of the studies presented to show that those strongly opposed to the death penalty were less likely to convict and those who supported the death penalty were more likely to convict. Justice Rehnquist, speaking for the majority, argued that, even if the justices did accept the validity of these studies, "the Constitution does not prohibit the States from 'death qualifying' juries in capital cases." Justice Rehnquist further observed,

… [T]he exclusion from jury service of large groups of individuals not on the basis of their inability to serve as jurors, but on the basis of some immutable (unchangeable) characteristic such as race, gender, or ethnic background, undeniably gave rise to an "appearance of unfairness."

[However], unlike blacks, women, and Mexican-Americans, "*Witherspoon*-excludables" are singled out for exclusion in capital cases on the basis of an attribute that is within the individual's control. It is important to remember that not all who oppose the death penalty are subject to removal for cause in capital cases; those who firmly believe that the death penalty is unjust may nevertheless serve as jurors in capital cases so long as they state clearly that they are willing to temporarily set aside their own beliefs in deference to the rule of law. Because the group of "*Witherspoon*-excludables" includes only those who cannot and will not conscientiously obey the law with respect to one of the issues in a capital case, "death qualification" hardly can be said to create an "appearance of unfairness."

Writing in dissent, Justice Marshall observed that if the High Court thought in *Witherspoon* that excluding those who opposed the death penalty meant that a convicted murderer would not get a fair hearing during the sentencing part of the trial, it would also logically mean that he or she would not get a fair hearing during the initial trial part. The Court minority generally accepted the studies showing "that 'death qualification' in fact produces juries somewhat more 'conviction-prone' than 'nondeath-qualified' juries."

JURY MAY CONSIDER A LESSER CHARGE

Along with an accomplice, Gilbert Beck entered the home of Roy Malone. While they were tying up the victim, Beck's accomplice unexpectedly struck and killed Malone. Beck admitted to the robbery, but claimed the murder was not part of the plan. Beck was tried under an Alabama statute for "robbery or attempts thereof when the victim is intentionally killed by the defendant."

Under Alabama law, the judge was specifically prohibited from giving the jury the option of convicting the defendant of a lesser included offense. Instead, the jury was given the choice of either convicting the defendant of the capital crime, in which case he possibly faced the death penalty, or acquitting him, thus allowing him to escape all penalties for his alleged participation in the crime. The judge could not have offered the jury the lesser alternative of felony-murder, which did not deal with the accused's intentions at the time of the crime.

Beck appealed, claiming this law created a situation in which the jury was more likely to convict. The Supreme Court, in *Beck v. Alabama* (447 U.S.

625, 1980), agreed and reversed the lower court's ruling. The High Court observed that, while not a matter of due process, it was virtually universally accepted in lesser offenses that a third alternative be offered. The Court noted,

That safeguard would seem to be especially important in a case such as this. For when the evidence unquestionably establishes that the defendant is guilty of a serious, violent offense — but leaves some doubt with respect to an element that would justify conviction of a capital offense — the failure to give the jury the "third option" of convicting on a lesser included offense would seem inevitably to enhance the risk of an unwarranted conviction.

According to the ruling, such a risk could not be tolerated in a case where the defendant's life was at stake. *Beck*, however, did not require a jury to consider a lesser charge in every case, but only where the consideration would be justified.

DOES THE BUCK STOP WITH THE JURY?

During the course of a robbery, Bobby Caldwell shot and killed the owner of a grocery store. He was tried and found guilty. During the sentencing phase of the trial, Caldwell's attorney pleaded for mercy, concluding his summation by emphasizing to the jury,

... I implore you to think deeply about this matter.... You are the judges and you will have to decide his fate. It is an awesome responsibility, I know — an awesome responsibility.

Responding to the defense attorney's plea, the prosecutor played down the responsibility of the jury, stressing the fact that a life sentence would be reviewed by a higher court.

[The defense] would have you believe that you're going to kill this man and they know ... that your decision is not the final decision.... Your job is reviewable.... [T]hey know, as I know, and as Judge Baker has told you, that the decision you render is automatically reviewable by the Supreme Court.

The jury sentenced Caldwell to death, and the case was automatically appealed. The Mississippi Supreme Court upheld the conviction, but split 4-4 on the validity of the death sentence, thereby upholding the death sentence by an equally divided court. Caldwell appealed to the U.S. Supreme Court.

In a 5-3 decision (Justice Powell took no part in the decision), the Supreme Court, in *Caldwell v. Mississippi* (472 U.S. 320, 1985), vacated (annulled) the death sentence. Writing for the majority, Justice Marshall noted,

> It is constitutionally impermissible to rest a death sentence on a determination made by a sentencer who has been led to believe that the responsibility for determining the appropriateness of the defendant's death rests elsewhere.... [This Court] has taken as a given that capital sentencers would view their task as the serious one of determining whether a specific human being should die at the hands of the State.

Furthermore, the High Court pointed out that the appeals court was not the place to make this life-and-death decision. Most appellate courts would presume that the sentencing was correctly done, which would leave the defendant at a distinct disadvantage. The jurors, expecting to be reversed by an appeals court, might choose to "send a message" of extreme disapproval of the defendant's acts and sentence him or her to death to show they will not tolerate such actions. Should the appeals court fail to reverse the decision, the defendant might be executed when the jury only intended to "send a message."

The three dissenting judges believed "the Court has overstated the seriousness of the prosecutor's comments" and that it was "highly unlikely that the jury's sense of responsibility was diminished."

KEEPING PAROLE INFORMATION FROM THE JURY

In 1990, Jonathan Dale Simmons beat an elderly woman to death in her home in Columbia, South Carolina. The week before his capital murder trial began, he pleaded guilty to first-degree burglary and two counts of criminal sexual conduct in connection with two prior assaults on elderly women. These guilty pleas resulted in convictions for violent offenses, which made him ineligible for parole if convicted of any other violent-crime offense.

At the capital murder trial, over the defense counsel's objection, the court did not allow the defense to ask prospective jurors if they understood the meaning of a "life" sentence as it applied to the defendant. Under South Carolina law, a defendant who was deemed a future threat to society and receiving a life sentence was ineligible for parole. The prosecution also asked the judge not to mention parole.

During deliberation, the jurors asked the judge if the imposition of a life sentence carried with it the possibility of parole. The judge told the jury,

> You are instructed not to consider parole or parole eligibility in reaching your verdict.... The terms life imprisonment and death sentence are to be understood in the plan [sic] and ordinary meaning....

The jury convicted Simmons of murder, sentencing him to death. On appeal, the South Carolina Supreme Court upheld the sentence. The case was brought before the U.S. Supreme Court. The High Court, in a 6-2 decision (*Simmons v. South Carolina* [512 U.S. 154, 1994]), overruled the South Carolina Supreme Court, concluding,

> Where a defendant's future dangerousness is at issue, and state law prohibits his re-

lease on parole, due process requires that the sentencing jury be informed that the defendant is parole ineligible. An individual cannot be executed on the basis of information which he had no opportunity to deny or explain…. Petitioner's jury reasonably may have believed that he could be released on parole if he were not executed. To the extent that this misunderstanding pervaded its deliberations, it had the effect of creating a false choice between sentencing him to death and sentencing him to a limited period of incarceration. The trial court's refusal to apprise the jury of information so crucial to its determination, particularly when the State alluded to the defendant's future dangerousness in its argument, cannot be reconciled with this Court's well-established precedents interpreting the Due Process Clause.

JUDGE SENTENCING INSTEAD OF JURY

Florida uses a trifurcated (three-part) trial system to deal with capital cases. The jury decides the guilt or innocence of the accused. If the jury finds the defendant guilty, it recommends an advisory opinion of either life imprisonment or the death sentence. The trial judge considers aggravating and mitigating circumstances, weighs them against the jury recommendation, and then sentences the convicted murderer to either life or death.

A Florida jury convicted Joseph Spaziano of torturing and murdering two women. The jury recommended that Spaziano be sentenced to life imprisonment, but the trial judge, after considering the mitigating and aggravating circumstances, sentenced the defendant to death. In his appeal, Spaziano claimed the judge's overriding of the jury's recommendation of life imprisonment violated the Eighth Amendment's prohibition against cruel and unusual punishment. The Supreme Court, in a 5-3 decision, in *Spaziano v. Florida* (468 U.S. 447, 1984), did not agree.

Spaziano's lawyers claimed juries, not judges, were better equipped to make reliable capital-sentencing decisions and that a jury's decision of life imprisonment should be inviolate (not questioned). They reasoned that the death penalty was unlike any other sentence and required that the jury have the ultimate word. This belief had been upheld, Spaziano claimed, because 30 out of 37 states with capital punishment had the jury decide the prisoner's fate. Furthermore, the primary justification for the death penalty was retribution and an expression of community outrage. The jury served as the voice of the community and knew best whether a particular crime was so terrible that the community's response must be the death sentence.

The High Court indicated that, although Spaziano's argument had some appeal, it contained two fundamental flaws. First, retribution played a role in all sentences, not just death sentences. Second, a jury was not the only source of community input. "The community's voice is heard at least as clearly in the legislature when the death penalty is authorized and the particular circumstances in which death is appropriate are defined." That trial judges imposed sentences was a normal part of the judicial system. The Supreme Court continued,

> In light of the facts that the Sixth Amendment does not require jury sentencing, that the demands of fairness and reliability in capital cases do not require it, and that neither the nature of, nor the purpose behind, the death penalty requires jury sentencing, we cannot conclude that placing responsibility on the trial judge to impose the sentence in a capital case is unconstitutional.

In addition, just because 30 of 37 states let the jury make the sentencing decision did not mean states that let a judge decide were wrong. The Court pointed out that there is no one right way for a state to establish its method of capital sentencing.

Writing for the dissenters, Justice Stevens indicated,

Because of its severity and irrevocability, the death penalty is qualitatively different from any other punishment, and hence must be accompanied by unique safeguards to ensure that it is a justified response to a given offense.... I am convinced that the danger of an excessive response can only be avoided if the decision to impose the death penalty is made by a jury rather than by a single governmental official ... [because a jury] is best able to "express the conscience of the community on the ultimate question of life or death."

Justice Stevens also gave weight to the fact that 30 out of 37 states had the jury make the decision, attesting to the "high level of consensus" (a majority view) that communities strongly believe life-or-death decisions should remain with the people — as represented by the jury — rather than relegated to a single government official.

Advisory Juries

Louise Harris asked a co-worker, Lorenzo McCarter, with whom she was having an affair, to find someone to kill her husband. McCarter paid two accomplices $100, with a vague promise of more money after they killed the husband. McCarter testified against Harris in exchange for the prosecutor's promise that he would not seek the death penalty against McCarter. McCarter testified that Harris had asked him to kill her husband so they could share in his death benefits. An Alabama jury convicted Louise Harris of capital murder. At the sentencing hearing, witnesses testified to her good background and strong character. She was rearing seven children, held three jobs simultaneously, and was active in her church.

Alabama law gives capital sentencing authority to the trial judge, but requires the judge to "consider" an advisory jury verdict. The jury voted 7 to 5 to give Harris life imprisonment without parole.

The trial judge then considered her sentence. He found one aggravating circumstance (the murder was committed for monetary gain), one statutory mitigating circumstance (Harris had no prior criminal record), and one nonstatutory mitigating circumstance (Harris was a hard-working, respected member of her church).

Noting that she had planned the crime, financed it, and stood to benefit from the murder, the judge felt that the aggravating circumstance outweighed the other mitigating circumstances and sentenced her to death. On appeal, the Alabama Supreme Court affirmed the conviction and sentence. It rejected Harris' arguments that the procedure was unconstitutional because Alabama state law did "not specify the weight the judge must give to the jury's recommendation and thus permits the arbitrary imposition of the death penalty."

On appeal, the U.S. Supreme Court upheld the Alabama court's decision (*Harris v. Alabama* [513 U.S. 504], 1995). Alabama's capital-sentencing process is similar to that of Florida (see *Spaziano* above). Both require jury participation during sentencing but give the trial judge the ultimate sentencing authority. However, while the Florida statute requires that a trial judge must give "great weight" to the jury recommendation, the Alabama statute requires only that the judge "considers" the jury's recommendation.

As in *Spaziano*, the High Court ruled that the Eighth Amendment does not require the State "to define the weight the sentencing judge must give to an advisory jury verdict."

Because the Constitution permits the trial judge, acting alone, to impose a capital sentence ... it is not offended when a State further requires a judge to consider a jury recommendation and trusts the judge to give it the proper weight....

CHAPTER III

LEGAL DECISIONS

CIRCUMSTANCES, RIGHT TO COUNSEL, EVIDENCE, AND VICTIM IMPACT STATEMENTS

RAPE AND KIDNAPPING DO NOT WARRANT DEATH

On June 20, 1977, a 5-4 divided Supreme Court ruled, in *Everheart v. Georgia* (433 U.S. 917) and in *Coker v. Georgia* (433 U.S. 584),

[R]ape is without doubt deserving of serious punishment, but in terms of moral depravity and of the injury to the person and to the public, it does not involve the unjustified taking of human life…. The murderer kills; the rapist, if no more than that, does not. Life is over for the victim of the murderers; for the rape victim, life may not be nearly so happy as it was, but it is not over and normally is not beyond repair. We have the abiding conviction that the death penalty, which is unique in its severity and irrevocability … is an excessive penalty for the rapist who, as such, does not take human life.

The Court also held that kidnapping did not warrant the death penalty. While the victims usually suffered tremendously, they had not lost their lives. (If the kidnapped victim were killed, then the kidnapper would be tried for murder.) These High Court decisions left only murder and treason as justifiable grounds for the imposition of the death penalty. So far, no cases involving the death penalty for treason have been brought to the Supreme Court.

MITIGATING CIRCUMSTANCES

Sandra Lockett was convicted for helping to plan and then driving the getaway car for a pawnshop robbery. Although it was unintended, the owner of the pawnshop was murdered. Lockett also hid her accomplices in her home. Later, she was tried for the capital murder of the pawnshop owner. According to the Ohio death penalty statute, capital punishment had to be imposed on Lockett unless "(1) the victim induced or facilitated the offense; (2) it is unlikely that the offense would have been committed but for the fact that the offender was under duress, coercion, or strong provocation; or (3) the offense was primarily the product of the offender's psychosis or mental deficiency." Lockett was found guilty and sentenced to die.

Lockett appealed, claiming that the Ohio law did not give the sentencing judge the chance to consider the circumstances of the crime and the defendant's character and record as mitigating (lessening the gravity of the crime) factors. In July 1978, the Supreme Court, in *Lockett v. Ohio* (438 U.S. 586), upheld Lockett's contention. Chief Justice Burger observed,

A statute that prevents the sentencer in capital cases from giving independent mitigating weights to aspects of the defendant's character and record and to the circumstances of the offense … creates the risk that the death penalty will be imposed in spite of factors that may call for a less severe penalty, and when the choice is between life and death, such risk is unacceptable and incompatible with the commands of the Eighth and Fourteenth Amendments.

Mitigating Circumstances Must Always Be Considered

In *Hitchcock v. Dugger* (481 U.S. 393, 1987), a unanimous Supreme Court further emphasized that all mitigating circumstances had to be considered before the convicted murderer could be sentenced. A Florida judge had instructed the jury not to consider, and he himself refused to consider, evidence of mitigating factors that were not specifically indicated in the Florida death penalty law. Writing for the Court, Justice Scalia stressed that a convicted person had the right "to present any and all relevant mitigating evidence that is available."

NOT BEING AT THE SCENE OF THE MURDER

On April 1, 1975, Sampson and Jeanette Armstrong, on the pretext of requesting water for their overheated car, tried to rob Thomas Kersey at home. Earl Enmund waited in the getaway car. Kersey called for his wife, who tried to shoot Jeanette Armstrong. The Armstrongs killed the Kerseys. Enmund was tried as an aider and abettor in the robbery-murder and sentenced to death.

In *Enmund v. Florida* (468 U.S. 782, 1982), a 5-4 split Supreme Court ruled that, in this case, the death penalty violated the Eighth and Fourteenth Amendments of the U.S. Constitution. The majority noted that only 9 of the 36 states with capital punishment permitted its use on a criminal who was not actually present at the scene of the crime. The exception was the case where someone paid a hitman to murder the victim.

Furthermore, over the years, juries had tended not to sentence to death criminals who had not actually been at the scene of the crime. Certainly

Enmund was guilty of planning and participating in a robbery, but murder had not been part of the plan. Since someone is killed in only 1 out of 200 robberies, Enmund could not have expected the Kerseys' murders during the robbery attempt. The Court concluded that, because Enmund did not kill or planned to kill, he should be tried only for his participation in the robbery. The Court observed,

We have no doubt that robbery is a serious crime deserving serious punishment. It is not, however, a crime "so grievous an affront to humanity that the only adequate response may be the penalty of death" [from *Gregg v. Georgia,* 428 U.S. 153, 1976]. It does not compare with murder, which does involve the unjustified taking of human life…. The murderer kills; the robber, if no more than that, does not. Life is over for the victim of the murderer; for the [robbery] victim, life … is not over and normally is not beyond repair.

Writing for the minority, Justice O'Connor concluded that intent is a complex issue. It should be left to the judge and jury trying the accused to decide intent, not a federal court far removed from the actual trial.

Enmund Reviewed

However, just because a person had no intent to kill does not mean that he or she cannot be sentenced to death. Crawford Bullock and a friend, Ricky Tucker, had been drinking at a bar. An acquaintance, Mark Dickson, offered them a ride home. During the drive, an argument ensued over money Dickson supposedly owed Tucker.

Outside the car, Bullock held Dickson while Tucker hit Dickson in the face with a whiskey bottle and punched him. When Dickson fell, Tucker smashed his head with a concrete block, killing him. Tucker and Bullock disposed of the body. The next day, police spotted Bullock driving the victim's car. After his arrest, Bullock confessed.

Under Mississippi law, a person involved in a robbery that results in murder may be convicted of capital murder regardless of "the defendant's own lack of intent that any killing take place." The jury never was asked to consider whether Bullock in fact killed, attempted to kill, or intended to kill. He was convicted and sentenced to death as an accomplice to the crime. During the appeals process, the Mississippi Supreme Court confirmed that Bullock was indeed a participant in the murder.

In January 1986, a 5-4 divided Supreme Court, in *Cabana v. Bullock* (474 U.S. 376), modified the *Enmund* decision. It indicated that while *Enmund* had to be considered at some point during the judicial process, the initial jury trying the accused did not necessarily have to consider the *Enmund* ruling. The High Court ruled that, while the jury had not been made aware of the issue of intent, the Mississippi Supreme Court had considered this question. Since *Enmund* did not require that *intent* be presented at the initial jury trial, only that it be considered at some time during the judicial process, the state of Mississippi had met that requirement.

The four dissenting justices claimed that it was difficult for any appeals court to determine intent from reading a typed transcript of a trial. It was important to see the accused and other involved individuals to help determine who was telling the truth and who was not. This was why *Enmund* must be raised to the jury so it could consider the question of intent in light of what it had seen and heard directly.

A "Reckless Indifference to the Value of Human Life" Is Just as Bad as Pulling the Trigger

Gary Tison was a convicted criminal who had been sentenced to life imprisonment for murdering a prison guard during an escape. Tison's three sons, his wife, his brother, and other relatives planned and carried out a prison escape involving Tison and a fellow prisoner, Randy Greenawalt, also a convicted murderer.

Tison's family provided Gary Tison and Greenawalt with guns. During the escape, their car had a flat tire, so they flagged down a passing car. The motorist who stopped to help was driving with his wife, their two-year-old son, and a 15-year-old niece.

Gary Tison then told his sons to go get some water from the motorist's car, presumably to be left with the family they planned to abandon in the desert. While the sons were gone, Gary Tison and Randy Greenawalt shot and killed the family. Several days later, two of Tison's sons and Greenawalt were captured. The third son was killed, and Tison escaped into the desert, where he later died of exposure.

The Tison sons and Greenawalt were found guilty and sentenced to death. The sons, citing *Enmund*, appealed, claiming that they had neither pulled the triggers nor intended the deaths of the family who had stopped to help them. The 5-4 Supreme Court decision (*Tison v. Arizona*, 481 U.S. 137, 1987) upheld the death sentence, indicating that the Tison sons had shown a "reckless indifference to the value of human life [which] may be every bit as shocking to the moral sense as an 'intent to kill.'"

The Tison sons may not have pulled the triggers (and the Court fully accepted the premise that they did not do the shootings or directly intend them to happen), but they released and then assisted two convicted murderers. They should have realized that freeing two killers and giving them guns could very well put innocent people in great danger. They continued to help the escapees even after the innocent family was killed.

"These facts," concluded Justice O'Connor for the majority, "not only indicate that the Tison [sons'] participation in the crime was anything but minor, they also would clearly support a finding that they both subjectively appreciated that their acts were likely to result in the taking of innocent life." Unlike the situation in the *Enmund* case, they were not sitting in a car far from the murder scene.

They were direct participants in the whole event. The death sentence would stand.

Writing for the minority, Justice Brennan observed that had a prison guard been murdered (Gary Tison had murdered a prison guard in a previous escape attempt), then the Court's argument would have made sense. However, the murder of the family made no sense and was not even necessary for the escape. The Tison sons were away from the murder scene getting water for the victims and could have done nothing to save them. While they were guilty of planning and carrying out an escape, the murder of the family who stopped to help them was an unexpected outcome of the escape.

Furthermore, the father had promised his sons that he would not kill during the escape, a promise he had kept despite several opportunities to kill during the actual prison escape. It was, therefore, not unreasonable for the sons not to have expected their father to kill in a situation that did not appear to warrant it. Justice Brennan concluded that "like Enmund, the Tisons neither killed nor attempted nor intended to kill anyone. Like Enmund, the Tisons have been sentenced to death for the intentional acts of others, which the Tisons did not expect, which were not essential to the felony, and over which they had no control."

AN "OUTRAGEOUSLY AND WANTONLY VILE" MURDER

Robert Godfrey and his wife of 28 years separated after a heated dispute. Mrs. Godfrey went to live with her mother, who supported her daughter's decision to leave her husband. During a telephone conversation, Mrs. Godfrey told her husband that reconciliation was impossible.

Later, Robert Godfrey took a shotgun and went to his mother-in-law's nearby trailer. He shot through a window, killing his wife instantly. He then entered the trailer, struck his fleeing daughter on the head with the gun, and shot his mother-in-law in the head, killing her. Godfrey then called the police, told them what he had done, and waited for the police to arrive.

The Georgia Code permits the imposition of the death penalty in the case of a murder that "was outrageously or wantonly vile, horrible, or inhuman in that it involved torture, depravity of mind, or an aggravated brutality to the victim." Aware of this law, the jury sentenced Godfrey to die. He appealed, claiming that the statute was unconstitutionally vague. After the Georgia Supreme Court upheld the lower court decision, the case was appealed to the U.S. Supreme Court.

The Supreme Court, in *Godfrey v. Georgia* (446 U.S. 420, 1980), noted that the victims were killed instantly (i.e., there was no torture), the victims had been "causing [Godfrey] extreme emotional trauma," and he acknowledged his responsibility. The High Court concluded that, in this case, the Georgia law was unconstitutionally vague. Moreover, the Georgia Supreme Court did not attempt to narrow the definition of "outrageously and wantonly vile." In a concurring opinion, Justice Marshall, whom Justice Brennan joined, found this an example of the inherently "arbitrary (subject to individual judgment) and capricious (unpredictable)" nature of capital punishment since even the prosecutor in Godfrey's case observed numerous times that there was no torture or abuse involved.

"COMPARATIVE PROPORTIONALITY REVIEW"

Robert Harris and his brother decided to steal a car they would need for a getaway in a planned bank robbery. Robert Harris approached two teenage boys eating hamburgers in a car. He forced them at gunpoint to drive to a nearby wooded area. The teenagers offered to delay telling the police of the car robbery and even to give the authorities misleading descriptions of the two robbers. When one of the boys appeared to be fleeing, Harris shot both of them. Harris and his brother later committed the robbery, were soon caught, and confessed to the robbery and murders.

Harris was found guilty. In California, a convicted murderer could only be sentenced to death or life imprisonment without parole if "special circumstances" existed and the murder had been "willful, deliberate, premeditated, and committed during the commission of kidnapping and robbery." This had to be proven during a separate sentencing hearing.

The state showed that Harris was convicted of manslaughter in 1975; he was found in possession of a make-shift knife and garrote (instrument used for strangulation) while in prison; he and other inmates sodomized another inmate; and he threatened that inmate's life. Harris testified that he had a very unhappy childhood, had little education, and his father had sexually molested his sisters. The jury sentenced Harris to death, and the judge concurred.

Harris claimed the U.S. Constitution, as interpreted in previous capital punishment rulings, required the state of California to give his case "comparative proportionality review" to determine if his death sentence was not out of line with others convicted of similar crimes. In "comparative proportionality review," a court considers the seriousness of the offense, the severity of the penalty, the sentences imposed for other crimes, and the sentencing in other jurisdictions for the same crime. Courts have occasionally struck down punishments inherently disproportionate and, therefore, cruel and unusual. Georgia, by law, and Florida, by practice, had incorporated such reviews in their procedures. Other states, such as Texas and California, had not.

After several appeals, the United States Ninth Circuit Court of Appeals agreed with Harris and ordered California to establish proportionality or lift the death sentence. The U.S. Supreme Court (*Pulley v. Harris*, 465 U.S. 37, 1984), in a 7-2 decision, did not agree. The Court noted that the California procedure contained enough safeguards to guarantee a defendant a fair trial and those convicted, a fair sentence. The High Court added,

That some [state statutes] providing proportionality review are constitutional does not mean that such review is indispensable.... To endorse the statute as a whole is not to say that anything different is unacceptable. Examination of our 1976 cases makes clear that they do not establish proportionality review as a constitutional requirement.

Justice Brennan, joined by Justice Marshall, dissented. He noted that the Supreme Court had thrown out the existing death penalty procedures during the 1970s because they were deemed arbitrary and capricious. He believed they still were, but the introduction of "proportionality" might "eliminate some, if only a small part, of the irrationality that currently surrounds the imposition of the death penalty."

WHEN DOES THE RIGHT TO COUNSEL END?

Joseph Giarratano was a Virginia prisoner under the sentence of death. He went to court, complaining that, because he was poor, the state of Virginia should provide him with a lawyer to help prepare conviction appeals. Virginia permitted condemned prisoners the right to use the prison libraries to prepare their appeals, but it did not provide the condemned with his own personal attorney.

Virginia had "unit attorneys" who were assigned to help prisoners with prison-related legal matters. A unit attorney could give guidance to death row inmates, but could not act as personal attorney for any one particular inmate. This case became a class action in which the federal district court certified a class comprising "all current and future Virginia inmates awaiting execution who do not have and cannot afford counsel to pursue post-conviction proceedings."

The federal district court and the federal court of appeals agreed with Giarratano, but the U.S. Supreme Court, in *Murray v. Giarratano* (492 U.S. 1, 1989), disagreed. Writing for the majority (Justices White, O'Connor, and Scalia, with Justice Kennedy filing a concurring opinion), Chief Justice Rehnquist concluded that, while the Sixth and Fourteenth Amendments of the U.S. Constitution assured an indigent (poor) defendant the right to counsel at the trial stage of a criminal proceeding, it does not provide for counsel for post-conviction proceedings, as they ruled in *Pennsylvania v. Finley* (481 U.S. 551, 1987). Since *Finley* had not specifically considered prisoners on death row, but all prisoners in general, the majority did not believe the decision needed to be reconsidered just because death row prisoners had more at stake.

Chief Justice Rehnquist agreed that those facing the death penalty had a right to counsel for the trial and during the initial appeal. During these periods, the defendant needed a heightened measure of protection because the death penalty was involved. Later appeals, however, involved more procedural matters that "serve a different and more limited purpose than either the trial or appeal."

In dissent, Justice Stevens (joined by Justices Brennan, Marshall, and Blackmun) indicated that he thought condemned prisoners in Virginia faced three critical differences from those considered in *Finley*. First, the Virginia prisoners had been sentenced to death, which makes their condition different from a sentence of life imprisonment. Second, Virginia's particular judicial decision forbids certain issues to be raised during the direct review or appeal process and forces them to be considered only during later post-conviction appeals. This means that very important issues may be considered without the benefit of counsel. Finally,

> ... Unlike the ordinary inmate, who presumably has ample time to use and reuse the prison library and to seek guidance from other prisoners experienced in preparing ... petitions, a grim deadline imposes a finite limit on the condemned person's capacity for useful research.... [As the district court concluded,] an inmate

preparing himself and his family for impending death is incapable of performing the mental functions necessary to adequately pursue his claims.

FEDERAL JUDGES CAN DELAY EXECUTIONS TO ALLOW *HABEAS* REVIEWS

A Texas jury found Frank McFarland guilty of stabbing to death a woman he had met in a bar. The appellate court upheld his conviction, and two lower federal courts refused his request for a stay (postponement) of execution. The federal courts ruled that they did not have jurisdiction to stop the execution until McFarland filed a *habeas corpus* (a prisoner's petition to be heard in federal court). The inmate argued that without the stay, he would be executed before he could obtain a lawyer to prepare the petition.

The Supreme Court granted a stay of execution. In a 5-4 decision (*McFarland v. Scott,* 512 U.S. 849, 1994), the Supreme Court ruled that federal law required governments to supply lawyers for poor defendants on death row who wanted to have *habeas* review. Once a defendant requested counsel, the federal court could postpone execution so the lawyer would have time to prepare an appeal. Justice Blackmun stated that "by providing indigent capital defendants with a mandatory right to qualified legal counsel in these proceedings, Congress has recognized that Federal *habeas corpus* has a particularly important role to play in promoting fundamental fairness in the imposition of the death penalty."

This case illustrated a problem in many states. For example, in 1994, there were 386 inmates on death row and only 118 lawyers with the Texas Resource Center, a federally financed legal office that handled capital cases. In 1993, judges in Texas set 100 execution dates. (State policy dictated that an execution must be scheduled about 45 days after the death sentence had been upheld on direct review.) If McFarland had drafted his own *habeas* petition, it would probably have been rejected as inadequate, and due to recent court rulings, an inmate has only one chance of filing a federal *habeas* petition.

HARMLESS ERROR*

Is Coerced Confession Harmless Error?

Oreste C. Fulminante called the Mesa, Arizona, police to report the disappearance of his 11-year-old stepdaughter, Jeneane Michelle Hunt. Fulminante was caring for the child while his wife, Jeneane's mother, was in the hospital. Several days later, Jeneane's body was found in the desert east of Mesa with two shots to the head, fired at close range by a large caliber weapon. There was a ligature (a cord used in tying or binding) around her neck. Because of the decomposed state of her body, it was not possible to determine whether she had been sexually assaulted.

Fulminante's statements about the child's disappearance and his relationship to her included inconsistencies that made him a suspect in her death. However, he was not charged with the murder. Fulminante left Arizona for New Jersey, where he was eventually convicted on federal charges of unlawful possession of a firearm by a felon.

While incarcerated, he became friendly with Anthony Sarivola, a former police officer. Sarivola had been involved in loansharking for organized crime, but then became a paid informant for the Federal Bureau of Investigation (FBI). In prison, he masqueraded as an organized crime figure. When Fulminante was getting some tough treatment from the other inmates, Sarivola offered him protection but only on the condition that Fulminante tell him everything.

Fulminante was later indicted in Arizona for the first-degree murder of Jeneane. In a hearing prior to the trial, Fulminante moved to suppress

(remove from the record) the statement he had made to Sarivola in prison and then later to Sarivola's wife, Donna, following his release from prison. He maintained that the confession to Sarivola was coerced, and that the second confession was the "fruit" of the first one.

The trial court denied the motion to suppress, finding that, based on the specified facts, the confessions were voluntary. Fulminante was convicted of Jeneane's murder and subsequently sentenced to death.

In his appeal, Fulminante argued, among other things, that his confession to Sarivola was coerced and that its use at the trial violated his rights of due process under the Fifth and Fourteenth Amendments of the U.S. Constitution. The Arizona Supreme Court ruled that the confession was coerced, but initially determined that the admission of the confession at the trial was a harmless error because of the overpowering evidence against Fulminante.

However, after Fulminante motioned for reconsideration, the Arizona Supreme Court ruled that the U.S. Supreme Court had set a precedent that prevented the use of harmless-error analysis in the case of a coerced confession. The Arizona Supreme Court reversed the conviction and ordered that Fulminante be retried without the use of the confession to Sarivola. Because of differences in the state and federal courts over the admission of a coerced confession with regard to harmless-error analysis, the U.S. Supreme Court agreed to hear the case.

In *Arizona v. Fulminante* (499 U.S. 279, 1991), Justice White, writing for the majority, stated that although the question was a close one, the Arizona Supreme Court was right in concluding that Fulminante's confession had been coerced. He further noted,

---

* The harmless-error standard, as stated in *Chapman v. California* (386 U.S. 18, 24; 1967), held that an error is harmless if it appears "beyond a reasonable doubt that the error complained of did not contribute to the verdict obtained."

The Arizona Supreme Court found a credible threat of physical violence unless Fulminante confessed. Our cases have [found] ... that a finding of coercion need not depend upon actual violence by a government agent; a credible threat is sufficient. As we have said, "coercion can be mental as well as physical, and ... the blood of the accused is not the only hallmark of an unconstitutional inquisition."

White further argued that the state of Arizona had failed to meet its burden of establishing, beyond a reasonable doubt, that the admission of Fulminante's confession to Sarivola was harmless. He wrote,

A defendant's confession is like no other evidence. Indeed, "the defendant's own confession is probably the most probative (providing evidence) that can be admitted against him.... [T]he admissions of a defendant come from the actor himself, the most knowledgeable and unimpeachable source of information about his past conduct. Certainly confessions have a profound impact on the jury, so much so that we may justifiably doubt its ability to put them out of mind even if told to do so" [From *Bruton v. United States*, 391 U.S. 123, 1968].

Presumption of Malice as Harmless Error

Dale Robert Yates and Henry Davis planned to rob a country store in Greenville County, South Carolina. When they entered the store, only the owner, Willie Wood, was present. Yates and Davis showed their weapons and ordered Wood to give them money from the cash register. Davis handed Yates the $3,000 and ordered Wood to lie across the counter. Wood, who had a pistol beneath his jacket, refused.

Meanwhile, Yates was backing out of the store with his gun pointed at the owner. After being told to do so by Davis, Yates fired two shots. The first bullet caused flesh wounds in Wood; the second shot missed. Yates then jumped into the car and waited for Davis. When Davis did not appear, he drove off. Inside the store, although wounded, Wood pursued Davis. As the two struggled, Wood's mother came in and ran to help her son. During the struggle, Mrs. Wood was stabbed once in the chest and died at the scene. Wood then shot Davis five times, killing him.

After Yates was arrested and charged with murder, his primary defense was that Mrs. Wood's death was not the probable natural consequence of the robbery he had planned with Davis. He claimed that he had brought the weapon only to induce the owner to give him the cash and that neither he nor Davis intended to kill anyone during the robbery.

The prosecutor's case for murder hinged on the agreement between Yates and Davis to commit an armed robbery. He argued that they planned to kill any witnesses, thereby making homicide a probable or natural result of the robbery. The prosecutor concluded, "[I]t makes no difference who actually struck the fatal blow, the hand of one is the hand of all."

In his instructions to the jury, the judge said,

Malice is implied or presumed by the law from the willful, deliberate and intentional doing of an unlawful act without any just cause or excuse. In its general signification, malice means the doing of a wrongful act, intentionally, without justification or excuse.... I tell you, also, that malice is implied or presumed from the use of a deadly weapon.

The judge continued to instruct the jury on the theory of accomplice liability. The jury returned guilty verdicts on the murder charge and on all other counts in the indictment. Yates was sentenced to death.

Yates petitioned the South Carolina Supreme Court, asserting that the jury charge that "malice is implied or presumed from the use of a deadly weapon" was an unconstitutional burden-shifting instruction. The case was twice reviewed by the South Carolina Supreme Court, which agreed that the jury instructions were unconstitutional, but that allowing the jury to presume malice was a harmless error (see footnote in *Fulminante* above). The state found that the jury did not have to rely on presumptions of malice because the fact that Davis "lunged" at Mrs. Wood and stabbed her were acts of malice.

The U.S. Supreme Court, in *Yates v. Evatt* (500 U.S. 391, 1991), reversed the decisions of the South Carolina Supreme Court and remanded the case (sent it back to the lower court for further proceedings). Justice Souter, writing for the High Court, ruled that the state supreme court failed to apply the proper harmless-error standard as stated in *Chapman*. "[T]he issue under *Chapman* is whether the jury actually rested its verdict on evidence establishing the presumed fact beyond a reasonable doubt, independently of the presumption."

Souter concluded by stating that there was clear evidence of Davis's attempt to kill Wood because he could have left the store with Yates, but stayed to pursue Wood with a deadly weapon. The evidence that Davis intended to kill Mrs. Wood was not as clear. The record also showed that Yates heard a woman scream as he left the store, but did not attempt to return and kill her.

The jury could have interpreted Yates's behavior to confirm his claim that he and Davis had not originally intended to kill anyone. Even the prosecutor, in summation, conceded that Mrs. Wood could have been killed inadvertently by Davis.

DUE PROCESS AND ADVANCE NOTICE OF IMPOSING THE DEATH PENALTY

Robert and Cheryl Bravence were beaten to death at their campsite near Santiam Creek, Idaho. Two brothers, Bryan and Mark Lankford, were charged with two counts of first-degree murder. At the arraignment (a summoning before a court

to hear and answer charges), the trial judge advised Bryan Lankford that, if convicted of either of the two charges (he was charged with both murders), the maximum punishment he might receive was either life imprisonment or death.

Following the arraignment, Bryan Lankford's attorney made a deal with the prosecutor to a plea bargain in which Bryan Lankford agreed to take two lie-detector tests. Although the results were somewhat unclear, they convinced the prosecutor that Lankford's older brother, Mark, was primarily responsible for the crimes and was the actual killer of both victims. Bryan Lankford's attorney and the prosecutor agreed on an indeterminate sentence with a 10-year minimum in exchange for a guilty plea, subject to commitment from the trial judge that he would impose that sentence. The judge refused to make such a commitment, and the case went to trial.

The judge refused to instruct the jury that a specific intent to kill was required to support a conviction of first-degree murder. The jury found Bryan Lankford guilty on both counts. The sentencing hearing was postponed until after Mark's trial. (He was also charged with both murders.)

Before the sentencing trial, at Bryan Lankford's request, the trial judge ordered the prosecutor to notify the court and Bryan Lankford whether it would seek the death penalty and, if so, to file a statement of the aggravating circumstance on which the death penalty would be based. The prosecutor notified the judge that the state would *not* recommend the death penalty. Several proceedings followed, including Lankford's request for a new attorney, a motion for a new trial, and a motion for continuance of the sentencing hearing. At none of the proceedings was there any mention that Lankford might receive the death penalty.

At the sentencing hearing, the prosecutor recommended a life sentence, with a minimum ranging between ten and 20 years. The trial judge indicated that he considered Lankford's testimony unbelievable and that the seriousness of the crime warranted more severe punishment than recommended by the state. He sentenced Lankford to death.

Lankford appealed, asserting that the trial judge violated the Constitution by failing to give notice he intended to impose the death penalty in spite of the state's earlier notice that it would not seek the death penalty. The judge maintained that Idaho Code provided Lankford with sufficient notice. The judge added that the fact the prosecutor said he would not seek the death penalty had "no bearing on the adequacy of notice to petitioner [Lankford] that the death penalty might be sought." The Idaho Supreme Court agreed with the judge's decision.

In *Lankford v. Idaho* (500 U.S. 110, 1991), the U.S. Supreme Court reversed the state supreme court ruling and remanded the case for a new trial. Writing for the majority, Justice Stevens stated that the due process clause of the Fourteenth Amendment was violated. Stevens noted,

> If the defense counsel had been notified that the trial judge was contemplating a death sentence based on five specific aggravating circumstances, presumably she would have advanced arguments that addressed these circumstances; however, she did not make these arguments because they were entirely inappropriate in a discussion about the length of the petitioner's possible incarceration.

Stevens further indicated that the trial judge's silence, in effect, hid from Lankford and his attorney, as well as from the prosecutor, the principal issues to be decided.

In a dissenting opinion, Justice Scalia wrote that Lankford's due process rights were not violated because he knew that he had been convicted of first-degree murder, and the Idaho Code clearly states that "every person guilty of murder of the first degree shall be punished by death or by imprisonment for life." At the arraignment, the trial judge told Lankford that he could receive either

punishment (see above). Scalia further noted that, in Idaho, the death penalty statute places full responsibility for determining the sentence on the judge.

EVIDENCE AND APPEALS

Newly Discovered Evidence Does Not Stop Execution

On an evening in late September 1981, the body of Texas Department of Public Safety Officer David Rucker was found lying beside his patrol car. He had been shot in the head. At about the same time, police officer Enrique Carrisalez saw a vehicle speeding away from the area where Rucker's body had been found. Carrisalez and his partner chased the vehicle and pulled it over. Carrisalez walked to the car. The driver opened his door and exchanged a few words with the police officer before firing at least one shot into Carrisalez's chest. The officer died nine days later.

Leonel Torres Herrera was arrested a few days after the shootings and charged with capital murder. In January 1982, he was tried and found guilty of murdering Carrisalez. In July 1982, he pleaded guilty to the murder of Rucker.

At the trial, Officer Carrisalez's partner identified Herrera as the person who fired the gun. He also testified that there was only one person in the car. In a statement by Carrisalez before he died, he also identified Herrera. The speeding car belonged to Herrera's girlfriend, and Herrera had the car keys in his pocket when he was arrested. Splatters of blood on the car and on Herrera's clothes were the same type as Rucker's. Strands of hair found in the car also belonged to Rucker. Finally, a handwritten letter, which strongly implied that he had killed Rucker, was found on Herrera when he was arrested

In 1992, 10 years after the initial trial, Herrera appealed to the federal courts, alleging that he was innocent of the murders of Rucker and Carrisalez and that his execution would violate the Eighth and

Fourteenth Amendments. He presented affidavits (sworn statements) claiming that he had not killed the officers, but that his now dead brother had. The brother's attorney, one of Herrera's cellmates, and a school friend all swore that the brother had killed the police officers. The dead brother's son also said that he had witnessed his father killing the men.

The U.S. Supreme Court, in *Herrera v. Collins* (506 U.S. 390, 1993), in a 7-3 decision, ruled that executing Herrera would not violate the Eighth and Fourteenth Amendments. The High Court said that the trial and not the appeals process judges guilt or innocence. Appeals courts only determine the fairness of the proceedings.

Writing for the majority, Chief Justice Rehnquist stated,

A person when first charged with a crime is entitled to a presumption of innocence and may insist that his guilt be established beyond a reasonable doubt.... Once a defendant has been afforded a fair trial and convicted of the offense for which he was charged, the presumption of innocence disappears.... Here, it is not disputed that the State met its burden of proving at trial that petitioner was guilty of the capital murder of Officer Carrisalez beyond a reasonable doubt. Thus, in the eyes of the law, petitioner does not come before the Court as one who is "innocent," but on the contrary as one who has been convicted by due process of two brutal murders.

Based on affidavits here filed, petitioner claims that evidence never presented to the trial court proves him innocent....

Claims of actual innocence based on newly discovered evidence have never been held to state a ground for [court] relief, absent an independent constitutional violation occurring in the underlying state criminal proceeding....

This rule is grounded in the principle that ... [appeals] courts sit to ensure that individuals are not imprisoned in violation of the Constitution — not to correct errors of fact....

Rehnquist continued that states all allow the introduction of new evidence. Texas is one of 17 states that require a new trial motion based on new evidence within 60 days. Herrera's appeal came 10 years later. However, the chief justice emphasized that Herrera still had options.

For under Texas law, petitioner may file a request for executive clemency. Executive clemency has provided the "fail safe" in our criminal justice system.... It is an unalterable fact that our judicial system, like the human beings who administer it, is fallible. But history is replete with examples of wrongfully convicted persons who have been pardoned in the wake of after-discovered evidence establishing their innocence.

The majority opinion found the information presented in the affidavits inconsistent with the other evidence. The justices questioned why the affidavits were produced at the very last minute. The justices also wondered why Herrera had pleaded guilty to the murder of Rucker if he had been innocent. They did note that some of the information in the affidavits might have been important to the jury, "but coming 10 years after the ... trial, this showing of innocence falls far short of that which would have to be made in order to trigger the sort of constitutional claim [to decide for a retrial]."

Speaking for the minority, Justice Blackmun wrote,

We really are being asked to decide whether the Constitution forbids the execution of a person who has been validly convicted and sentenced but who, nonetheless, can prove his innocence with newly discovered evidence. Despite the State of Texas' astonishing protestation to the contrary ... I do not see how the answer can be anything but "yes."

The Eighth Amendment prohibits "cruel and unusual punishments." This proscription (prohibition) is not static (fixed) but rather reflects evolving standards of decency. I think it is crystal clear that the execution of an innocent person is "at odds with contemporary standards of fairness and decency" .... The protection of the Eighth Amendment does not end once a defendant has been validly convicted and sentenced.

Claim of Miscarriage of Justice

Lloyd Schlup, a Missouri prisoner, was convicted of participating in the murder of a fellow inmate and sentenced to death. He had filed one petition for *habeas corpus*, arguing that he had inadequate counsel. He filed a second petition, alleging that constitutional error at his trial deprived the jury of crucial evidence that would have established his innocence.

Using a previous U.S. Supreme Court ruling (*Sawyer v. Whitley*, 505 U.S. 333, 1992), the district court claimed that Schlup had not shown "by clear and convincing evidence that, but for a constitutional error, no reasonable juror would have found him guilty." Schlup's lawyers argued that the district court should have used another ruling (*Murray v. Carrier*, 477 U.S. 478, 1986), in which a petitioner need only to show that "a constitutional violation has probably resulted in the conviction of one who is actually innocent." The appellate court affirmed the district court's ruling, noting that Schlup's guilt, which had been proven at the trial, barred any consideration of his constitutional claim.

The U.S. Supreme Court, upon appeal, reviewed the case to determine whether the *Sawyer* standard provides enough protection from a miscarriage of justice that would result from the ex-

ecution of an innocent person. In *Schlup v. Delo* (513 U.S. 298, 1995), the Court observed,

[I]f a petitioner such as Schlup presents evidence of innocence so strong that a court cannot have confidence in the outcome of the trial unless the court is also satisfied that the trial was free of non-harmless constitutional error, the petitioner should be allowed to ... argue the merits of his underlying claims.

The justices concluded that the *Carrier*, rather than *Sawyer*, standard focuses the investigation on the actual innocence, allowing the Court to review relevant evidence that might have been excluded or unavailable during the trial.

Suppressed Evidence Means a New Trial

Curtis Lee Kyles was convicted by a Louisiana jury of the first-degree murder of a woman in a grocery store parking lot in 1984. He was sentenced to death. It was revealed on review that the prosecutor had never disclosed certain evidence favorable to the defendant. The state supreme court, the federal district court, and the Fifth Circuit Court denied Kyles' appeals. The U.S. Supreme Court, in *Kyles v. Whitley* (514 U.S, 419, 1995), reversed the lower courts' decisions. The High Court ruled,

Favorable evidence is material, and constitutional error results from its suppression by the government, if there is a "reasonable probability" that, had the evidence been disclosed to the defense, the result of the proceeding would have been different.... [The] net effect of the state-suppressed evidence favoring Kyles raises a reasonable probability that disclosure would have produced a different result at trial.

The conviction was overturned. Four mistrials followed. On February 18, 1998, after his fifth and final trial ended with a hung jury, Curtis Lee Kyles was released from death row.

VICTIM IMPACT STATEMENTS

First, They Are Not Constitutional

John Booth and Willie Reid stole money from elderly neighbors to buy heroin. Booth, knowing his neighbors could identify him, tied up the elderly couple and then repeatedly stabbed them in the chest with a kitchen knife. The couple's son found their bodies two days later. Booth and Reid were found guilty.

The state of Maryland permitted a victim impact statement (VIS) to be read to the jury during the sentencing phase of the trial. The VIS prepared in this case explained the tremendous pain caused by the murder of the parents and grandparents to the family. It revealed that not only had the murdered victims suffered, but their family also suffered severely in many ways, including sleepless nights, lack of trust, depression, and disorientation. A 5-4 Supreme Court, in *Booth v. Maryland* (482 U.S. 496, 1987), while recognizing the agony caused to the victim's family, ruled that victim impact statements, as required by Maryland's statute, were unconstitutional and could not be used during the sentencing phase of a capital murder trial.

Writing for the majority, Justice Powell indicated that a jury must determine whether the defendant should be executed, based on the circumstances of the crime and the character of the offender. These factors had nothing to do with the victim. The High Court noted that it is the crime and the criminal that were at issue. Had Booth and Reid viciously murdered a drunken bum, the crime would have been just as horrible.

Furthermore, some families could express the pain and disruption they suffered as a result of the murder better than other families. Should a sentencing be dependent upon how well a family could express its grief? In addition, if the character of the victim should play a role in determining the sentence, then the prisoner should have the right to attack that character to show it was not as flaw-less as presented. This could likely lead to attacks on the character of the victim and more pain for the victim's family.

... And Then They Are

Pervis Tyronne Payne spent the morning and early afternoon injecting cocaine and drinking beer. Later, he drove around the town with a friend, each of them taking turns reading a pornographic magazine. In mid-afternoon, Payne went to his girlfriend's apartment across the hall from the apartment of Charisse Christopher. He entered the Christophers' apartment and made sexual advances toward Charisse, who resisted. Payne became violent.

The first police officer to arrive at the scene saw Payne leaving the building so covered with blood that he appeared to be "sweating blood." Inside the apartment, the police saw Charisse and her children lying on the kitchen floor. Blood covered the walls and floor throughout the apartment.

Charisse had 42 direct knife wounds and 42 defensive wounds on her arms and hands. The two-year-old daughter had suffered stab wounds to the chest, abdomen, back, and head. The murder weapon, a butcher knife, was found at her feet. Charisse's three-year-old son, despite several stab wounds that went completely through his body, was still alive. Payne was arrested, and a Tennessee jury convicted Payne of the first-degree murders of Charisse Christopher and her daughter, and of the first-degree assault, with intent to murder, of Charisse's son, Nicholas.

During the sentencing phase of the trial, Payne called his parents, his girlfriend, and a clinical psychologist to testify about the mitigating aspects of his background and character. The prosecutor, on the other hand, called Nicholas's grandmother, who testified how much the child missed his mother and baby sister. In arguing for the death penalty, the prosecutor commented on the continuing effects the crime had had on Nicholas and his family. The jury sentenced Payne to death on each of the murder counts. The state supreme court agreed, rejecting Payne's claim that the admission of the grandmother's testimony and the state's closing argument violated his Eighth Amendment rights under *Booth v. Maryland* (see above).

On hearing the appeal (*Payne v. Tennessee*, 501 U.S. 808, 1991), a 6-3 U.S. Supreme Court upheld the death penalty and overturned both *Booth v. Maryland* and *South Carolina v. Gathers* (490 U.S. 805, 1989; in *Gathers*, the Court reversed the defendant's death sentence because of the prosecutor's statement about the victim being a religious man and a registered voter). In *Payne*, the Court ruled that the Eighth Amendment does not prohibit a jury from considering, at the sentencing phase of a capital trial, victim impact evidence relating to a victim's personal characteristics and the emotional impact of the murder on the victim's family. The Eighth Amendment also does not bar a prosecutor from arguing such evidence at the sentencing phase.

The Court reasoned that the assessment of harm caused by a defendant as a result of a crime has long been an important concern of criminal law in determining both the elements of the offense and the appropriate punishment. Victim impact evidence is simply another form or method of informing the sentencing jury or judge about the specific harm caused by the crime in question.

The *Booth* case unfairly weighted the scales in a capital trial. No limits were placed on the mitigating evidence the defendant introduced relating to his own circumstances. However, the state was barred from offering a glimpse of the life, which the defendant chose to extinguish or from showing the loss to the victim's family or to society. *Booth* and *Gathers* were decided by narrow mar-

gins, the Court continued, and had been questioned by members of the Supreme Court as well as by the lower courts.

Chief Justice Rehnquist, delivering the opinion of the Court, stated,

… The State has a legitimate interest in counteracting the mitigating evidence which the defendant is entitled to put in, by reminding the sentencer that just as the murderer should be considered as an individual, so too the victim is an individual whose death represents a unique loss to society and in particular to his family.

Justice Stevens, dissenting, stated,

[A victim impact statement] sheds no light on the defendant's guilt or moral culpability (blameworthiness) and thus serves no purpose other than to encourage jurors to decide in favor of death rather than life on the basis of their emotions rather than their reason.

Victim impact evidence, as used in this case, has two flaws. First, aspects of the character of the victim, unforeseeable to the defendant at the time of his crime, are irrelevant to the defendant's "personal responsibility and moral guilt" and therefore cannot justify a death sentence....

Second, the quantity and quality of victim impact evidence sufficient to turn a verdict of life in prison into a verdict of death is not defined until after the crime has been committed and therefore cannot possibly be applied consistently in different cases.

CHAPTER IV

LEGAL DECISIONS

YOUTH, INSANITY, RACE, AND METHODS OF EXECUTION

CAN A MINOR BE SENTENCED TO DEATH?

On April 4, 1977, 16-year-old Monty Lee Eddings and several friends were pulled over by a police officer as they traveled in a car. Eddings had several guns in the car, which he had taken from his father. When the police officer approached the car, Eddings shot and killed him. Eddings was tried as an adult even though he was 16 at the time of the murder. He was convicted of first-degree murder for killing a police officer and was sentenced to death.

At the sentencing hearing following the conviction, Eddings' lawyer presented substantial evidence of a turbulent family history, beatings by a harsh father, and serious emotional disturbance. The judge refused, as a matter of law, to consider the mitigating (lessening the gravity of the crime) circumstances of Eddings' unhappy upbringing and emotional problems. He ruled that the only mitigating circumstance was the petitioner's youth, which was insufficient to outweigh the aggravating circumstances.

In *Eddings v. Oklahoma* (455 U.S. 104, 1982), the Supreme Court, in a 5-4 opinion, ordered the case remanded (sent back to the lower courts for further proceedings). The justices based their ruling on *Lockett v. Ohio* (438 U.S. 586, 1978), which required the trial court to consider and weigh all of the mitigating evidence concerning the petitioner's family background and personal history.

By implication, since the majority did not reverse the case on the issue of age, it let stand Oklahoma's decision to try Eddings as an adult. Meanwhile, Chief Justice Warren Burger, who filed the dissenting opinion in which Justices White, Blackmun, and Rehnquist joined, observed,

... [T]he Constitution does not authorize us to determine whether sentences imposed by state courts are sentences we consider "appropriate"; our only authority is to decide whether they are constitutional under the Eighth Amendment. The Court stops far short of suggesting that there is any constitutional proscription (prohibition) against imposition of the death penalty on a person who was under age 18 when the murder was committed.

Hence, while the High Court did not directly rule on the question of minors being sentenced to death, the sense of the court would appear to be that it would uphold such a sentencing.

Not at Fifteen Years Old

With three adults, William Thompson brutally murdered a former brother-in-law. Thompson was 15 at the time of the murder, but the state determined that Thompson, who had a long history of violent assault, had "virtually no *reasonable* prospects for rehabilitation ... within the juvenile system and ... should be held accountable for his acts as if he were an adult and should be certified to stand trial as an adult." Thompson was tried as an adult and found guilty. As in *Eddings* (see above), his age was considered a mitigating circumstance, but the jury still sentenced him to death.

Thompson appealed, and while the Court of Criminal Appeals of Oklahoma upheld the decision, the U.S. Supreme Court, in *Thompson v. Oklahoma* (487 U.S. 815, 1988), did not. In a 5-3 majority vote, with Justice O'Connor agreeing to vacate (annul) the sentence, but not agreeing with the majority reasoning, the case was reversed. (Justice Kennedy took no part in the decision.)

Writing for the majority (Justices Stevens, Brennan, Marshall, and Blackmun), Justice Stevens observed,

> Inexperience, less education, and less intelligence make the teenager less able to evaluate the consequences of his or her conduct, while at the same time he or she is much more apt to be motivated by mere emotion or peer pressure than is an adult. The reasons why juveniles are not trusted with the privileges and responsibilities of an adult also explain why their irresponsible conduct is not as morally reprehensible (blameworthy) as that of an adult.

Justice Stevens noted that 18 states required the age of at least 16 years before the death penalty could be considered. Counting the 14 states prohibiting capital punishment, a total of 32 states did not execute people under 16.

Justice O'Connor agreed with the judgment of the Court that the appellate court's ruling should be reversed. However, O'Connor pointed out that, although most 15-year-old criminals are generally less blameworthy than adults who commit the same crimes, some may fully understand the horrible deeds they have done. Individuals, after all, have different characteristics, including their capability to distinguish right from wrong.

Writing for the minority (Justices Scalia, Rehnquist, and White), Justice Scalia found no national consensus forbidding the execution of a person who was 16 at the commission of the murder. The justice could not understand the majority's calculations establishing a "contemporary standard" that forbade the execution of young minors. Abolitionist states (those states that did not have the death penalty) should not be considered in the issue of executing minors since they did not have executions in the first place. Rather, the 18 states that prohibited the execution of offenders who were younger than 16 when they murdered should be compared to the 19 states that applied the death penalty to young offenders.

But It May Be Done at 16

A majority of the Court, with Justice O'Connor straddling the fence, found the death penalty unacceptable for an offender who was less than 16 when he or she committed murder. However, a majority of the Court found the death sentence acceptable for a minor who was 16 or 17 during the commission of murder. The Supreme Court, in two jointly considered cases, *Stanford v. Kentucky* and *Wilkins v. Missouri* (492 U.S. 361, 1989), ruled that juveniles ages 16 and 17 could be executed for murder.

When he was 17 years old, Kevin Stanford and an accomplice raped the attendant at a gas station they were robbing. They then took the woman to a secluded area near the station, where Stanford shot her in the face and in the back of her head. Stressing the seriousness of the offense and Stanford's long history of criminal behavior, the Court certified him as an adult. He was tried, found guilty, and sentenced to death.

When he was 16 years old, Heath Wilkins stabbed Nancy Allen to death while he was robbing the convenience store where she worked. Wilkins indicated he murdered Allen because "a dead person can't talk." Based on his long history of juvenile delinquency, the Court ordered Wilkins tried as an adult. He was found guilty and sentenced to die.

Writing for the majority (Justices Scalia, Rehnquist, White, and Kennedy), Justice Scalia could find no national consensus that executing minors ages 16 and 17 constituted cruel and unusual punishment. Scalia observed that of the 37 States whose statutes allowed the death penalty, just 15 refused to impose it on 16-year-old offenders and 12 states, on 17-year-old offenders.

Further, Justice Scalia saw no connection between the defendant's argument that those under 18 were denied the right to drive, drink, or vote because they were not considered mature enough to do so responsibly and whether this standard of maturity should be applied to a minor's understanding that murder is terribly wrong. Scalia added,

> [E]ven if the requisite degrees of maturity were comparable, the age statutes in question would still not be relevant. These laws set the appropriate ages for the operation of a system that makes its determinations in gross, and that does not conduct individualized maturity tests for each driver, drinker, or voter. The criminal justice system, however, does provide individualized testing. In the realm of capital punishment in particular, "individualized consideration [is] a constitutional requirement," ... and one of the individualized mitigating factors that sentencers must be permitted to consider is the defendant's age.

Justice O'Connor also concluded that no national consensus prohibited the imposition of the death penalty on Stanford and Wilkins. However, O'Connor believed that the High Court had the constitutional obligation to determine whether the punishment imposed was proportional to the defendants' blameworthiness.

Writing for the minority (Justices Brennan, Marshall, Blackmun, and Stevens), Justice Brennan found a national consensus among 30 states when he added the 12 states forbidding the execution of a person who was 16 years during the commission of the crime, those with no capital punishment, and the states that, in practice, did not execute minors. Justice Brennan, taking serious exception to the majority's observation that they had to find a national consensus in the laws passed by the state legislatures, stated,

> Our judgment about the constitutionality of a punishment under the Eighth Amendment is informed, though not determined ... by an examination of contemporary attitudes toward the punishment, as evidenced in the actions of legislatures and of juries. The views of organizations with expertise in relevant fields and the choices of governments elsewhere in the world also merit our attention as indicators whether a punishment is acceptable in a civilized society.

Youth — A Mitigating Circumstance

Dorsie Lee Johnson Jr., age 19, and an accomplice staked out a convenience store, with the intention of robbing it. They found out that only one employee worked during the predawn hours. Agreeing to leave no witnesses to their crime, Johnson shot and killed the clerk, Jack Huddleston. They then emptied the cash register and stole some cigarettes.

The following month, Johnson was arrested and subsequently confessed to the murder and the robbery. During the jury selection, the defense attorneys asked potential jurors whether they believed that people were capable of change and whether they, the potential jurors, had ever done things in their youth that they would not now do.

The only witness the defense called was Johnson's father, who told of his son's drug use, grief over the death of his mother two years before the crime, and the murder of his sister the following year. He especially talked of his son's youth and the fact that, at age 19, he did not evaluate things the way a person of 30 or 35 would.

Johnson was tried and convicted of capital murder. Under Texas law, the homicide qualified as a capital offense because Johnson intentionally or knowingly caused Huddleston's death. Moreover, the murder was carried out in the course of committing a robbery.

In the sentencing phase of the trial, the judge instructed the jury to answer two questions: (1) whether Johnson's actions were deliberate and intended to kill, and (2) whether there was a possibility that he would continue to commit violent crimes and be a threat to society. If the jury answered "yes" to both questions, Johnson would be sentenced to death. If the jury returned a "no" answer to either question, the defendant would be sentenced to life in prison. The jury was not to consider or discuss the possibility of parole.

Of equal importance was the instruction that the jury could consider all the evidence, both aggravating and mitigating, in either phase of the trial. The jury unanimously answered yes to both questions, and Johnson was sentenced to death.

Five days after the state appellate court denied Johnson's motions for a rehearing, the U.S. Supreme Court issued its opinion in another case, *Penry v. Lynaugh* (492 U.S. 302, 1989) (see below). Based on the *Penry* ruling, Dorsie Lee Johnson claimed that a separate instruction should have been given to the jury that would have allowed them to consider his youth. Again, the appellate court rejected Johnson's petition.

Affirming the Texas appellate court decision, Justice Kennedy delivered the opinion of the Supreme Court in *Johnson v. Texas* (509 U.S. 350, 1993). He was joined by Justices Rehnquist, White, Scalia, and Thomas. Kennedy noted that the Texas special-issues system (two questions asked of the jury and instruction to consider all evidence) allowed for adequate consideration of Johnson's youth. Justice Kennedy stated,

Even on a cold record, one cannot be unmoved by the testimony of petitioner's father urging that his son's actions were due in large part to his youth. It strains credu-

lity to suppose that the jury would have viewed the evidence of petitioner's youth as outside its effective reach in answering the second special issue. The relevance of youth as a mitigating factor derives from the fact that the signature qualities of youth are transient; as individuals mature, the impetuousness and recklessness that may dominate in younger years can subside.... As long as the mitigating evidence is within "the effective reach of the sentencer," the requirements of the Eighth Amendment are satisfied.

Justice O'Connor, in a dissenting opinion joined by Justices Blackmun, Stevens, and Souter, stated that the jurors were not allowed to give "full effect to his strongest mitigating circumstance: his youth." Hearing of his less than exemplary youth, a jury might easily conclude, as Johnson's did, that he would continue to be a threat to society.

ROLE OF PSYCHIATRISTS

Is the Testimony of a Psychiatrist Valid?

In 1978, Thomas Barefoot was convicted of murdering a police officer. During the sentencing phase of the trial, the prosecution put two psychiatrists on the stand. Neither psychiatrist had actually interviewed Barefoot nor did either ask to do so. Both psychiatrists agreed that an individual with Barefoot's background and who had acted as Barefoot had in murdering the policeman represented a future threat to society. Partially based on their testimony, the jury sentenced Barefoot to death.

Barefoot's conviction and sentence were appealed numerous times, and in 1983, his case was argued before the U.S. Supreme Court. Among the issues debated was the validity of the testimony of psychiatrists. Barefoot's lawyers questioned whether it was necessary for the psychiatrists to have interviewed Barefoot or if it was enough for them to answer hypothetical questions that pertained to a hypothetical individual who acted like Barefoot.

Barefoot's attorneys claimed that psychiatrists could not reliably predict that a particular offender would commit other crimes in the future and be a threat to society. They further argued that psychiatrists should also not be allowed to testify about an offender's future dangerousness in response to hypothetical situations presented by the prosecutor and without having first examined the offender.

In *Barefoot v. Estelle* (463 U.S. 880, 1983), the 6-3 Supreme Court ruled that local juries were in the best position to decide guilt and impose a sentence. The Court referred to *Jurek v. Texas* (428 U.S. 262, 1976, see Chapter II), an earlier case that, among other things, upheld the testimony of lay persons concerning a defendant's possible future actions. The Court, therefore, looked upon psychiatrists as just another group of people presenting testimony to the jury for consideration. Like all evidence presented to the jury, the Court claimed,

> [A psychiatric observation] should be admitted and its weight left to the fact finder, who would have the benefit of cross examination and contrary evidence by the opposing party. Psychiatric testimony predicting dangerousness may be countered not only as erroneous in a particular case but as generally so unreliable that it should be ignored. If the jury may make up its mind about future dangerousness unaided by psychiatric testimony, jurors should not be barred from hearing the views of the State's psychiatrists along with opposing views of the defendant's doctors.

The High Court dismissed the *amicus* brief (a friend-of-the-court brief prepared to enlighten the court) presented by the American Psychiatric Association (APA), indicating that psychiatric testimony was "almost entirely unreliable" in determining future actions. The Court countered that such testimony had been traditionally accepted. The Court also observed that arguments, such as the APA *amicus* brief, were founded "on the premise that a jury will not be able to separate the wheat from the chaff," a sentiment the Court did not agree with.

The High Court also dismissed Barefoot's contention that the psychiatrists should have personally interviewed him. Such methods of observation and conclusion were quite normal in courtroom procedures and the psychiatric observations had been based on established facts. Barefoot's appeal was denied.

Justice Blackmun strongly dissented from the majority decision. He declared,

> In the present state of psychiatric knowledge, this is too much for me. One may accept this in a routine lawsuit for money damages, but when a person's life is at stake — no matter how heinous his offense — a requirement of greater reliability should prevail.... In a capital case, the specious (seemingly fair but not so) testimony of a psychiatrist, colored in the eyes of an impressionable jury by the inevitable untouchability of a medical specialist's words, equates with death itself.

A Prisoner Maintains Rights
Before a Psychiatrist

During the commission of a robbery, Ernest Smith's accomplice fatally shot a grocery clerk (Smith had tried to shoot the clerk, but his weapon had jammed). The state of Texas sought the death penalty against Smith based on the Texas law governing premeditated murder.

Thereafter, the judge ordered a psychiatric examination of Smith by Dr. James Grigson to determine if Smith was competent to stand trial. Without permission from Smith's lawyer, Dr. Grigson interviewed Smith in jail for about 90 minutes and found him competent. Dr. Grigson then discussed his conclusions and diagnosis with the state attorney. Smith was found guilty. During the sentencing phase of the trial, over the protests of the defendant's lawyers, Grigson testified that Smith was a "very severe sociopath," who would continue his previous behavior, which would get worse. The jury sentenced Smith to death.

Smith appealed his sentence, claiming he was not informed of his rights. Both the federal district court and the appeals court agreed. So did a unanimous 9-0 Supreme Court. In *Estelle v. Smith* (451 U.S. 454, 1981), the Court ruled that the trial court had the right to determine if Smith was capable of standing trial. However, it had no right to use the information gathered without first advising him of his Fifth Amendment right. Noting *Miranda v. Arizona* (384 U.S. 436, 1966), the Court continued,

> The Fifth Amendment privilege is available outside of criminal court proceedings and serves to protect persons in all settings in which their freedom of action is curtailed in any significant way from being compelled to incriminate themselves.... The prosecution may not use statements, whether exculpatory (proving innocence) or inculpatory (incriminating), stemming from custodial (while under arrest) interrogation of the defendant unless it demonstrates the use of procedural safeguards effective to secure the privilege against self-incrimination.

Needing a Psychiatrist to Prove Insanity

In 1979, Glen Burton Ake and Steven Hatch shot and killed Reverend and Mrs. Richard Douglass and wounded their children, Brooks and Leslie. Before the trial, due to Ake's bizarre behavior, the trial judge ordered that he be examined by a psychiatrist to determine if he should be put under observation. The psychiatrist diagnosed Ake as a probable paranoid schizophrenic and recommended a long-term psychiatric examination to determine his competency to stand trial.

Ake's psychiatric evaluation confirmed his paranoid schizophrenia. Consequently, the court pronounced him incompetent to stand trial and ordered him committed to the state mental hospital.

Six weeks later, the hospital psychiatrist informed the Court that Ake had become competent to stand trial. Under daily treatment with an anti-psychotic drug, he could stand trial. The state of Oklahoma resumed proceedings against the accused murderer.

Prior to the trial, Ake's lawyer told the Court of his client's insanity defense. He also informed the Court that in order for him to adequately defend Ake, he needed to have Ake examined by a psychiatrist to determine his mental condition at the time he committed murder. During his stay at the mental hospital, Ake was evaluated as to his "present sanity" to stand trial but not his mental state during the murder. Since Ake could not afford a psychiatrist, his counsel asked the Court to provide a psychiatrist or the money to hire one. The trial judge refused his request, claiming the state is not obligated to provide a psychiatrist, even to poor defendants in capital cases.

Ake was tried for two counts of first-degree murder and for two counts of shooting with intent to kill. During the trial, Ake's only defense was insanity; however, none of the psychiatrists at the state mental hospital could testify to his mental state at the time of the crime. *As a result, there was no expert testimony for either side on Ake's sanity at the time of the offense.* (Italics are from the release of the Supreme Court. See below.)

The judge instructed the jurors that Ake could be found not guilty by reason of insanity if he could not distinguish right from wrong when he committed murder. The jurors were told they could presume Ake sane at the time of the crime unless he presented sufficient evidence to raise a reasonable doubt about his sanity at the time of the crime. The jury found him guilty on all counts. The jury sentenced Ake to death based on the earlier testimony of the psychiatrist who concluded he was a threat to society. Upon appeal, the Oklahoma Court of Appeals agreed with the trial court that the state did not have the responsibility to provide an indigent (poor) defendant with a psychiatrist to help with his defense.

The U.S. Supreme Court disagreed. In an 8-1 ruling, the Court, in *Ake v. Oklahoma* (470 U.S.

68, 1985), reversed the lower court's ruling. The High Court observed,

> This Court has long recognized that when a State brings its judicial power to bear on an indigent defendant in a criminal proceeding, it must take steps to assure that the defendant has a fair opportunity to present his defense. This elementary principle, grounded in significant part on the Fourteenth Amendment's due process guarantee of fundamental fairness, derives from the belief that justice cannot be equal where, simply as a result of his poverty, a defendant is denied the opportunity to participate meaningfully in a judicial proceeding in which his liberty is at stake....

CAN AN INSANE PERSON BE EXECUTED?

In 1974, Alvin Ford was convicted of murder and sentenced to death. There was no question that he was completely sane at the time of his crime, at the trial, and at the sentencing. Eight years later, Ford began to show signs of delusion — from thinking that people were conspiring to force him to commit suicide to believing that family members were being held hostage in prison.

Ford's lawyers had a psychiatrist examine their client. After 14 months of evaluation and investigation, the doctor concluded that Ford suffered from a severe mental disorder that would preclude him from assisting in the defense of his life. A second psychiatrist concluded that Ford did not understand why he was on death row.

Florida law required the governor to appoint a panel of three psychiatrists to determine whether Ford was mentally capable of understanding the death penalty and the reasons why he was being sentenced to death. The three state-appointed doctors met with Ford once for about 30 minutes and then filed separate reports. Ford's lawyers were present but were ordered by the judge not to participate in the examination "in any adversarial manner."

The three psychiatrists submitted different diagnoses, but all agreed that Ford was sane enough to be executed. Ford's lawyers attempted to submit the reports of the first two psychiatrists along with other materials. The governor, refusing to inform the lawyers whether he would consider these reports, proceeded to sign Ford's death warrant.

Ford's appeals were denied in state and federal courts, but a 7-2 Supreme Court, in *Ford v. Wainwright* (477 U.S. 399, 1986), reversed the earlier judgments. Writing for the majority, Justice Marshall observed that, while the reasons appear unclear, English common law forbade the execution of the insane. The English jurist William Blackstone (1723-1780) had labeled such a practice "savage and inhuman." Likewise, the other noted English judicial resource, Sir Edward Coke (1552-1634), observed that, while the execution of a criminal was to serve as an example, the execution of a madman was considered "of extreme inhumanity and cruelty, and can be no example to others." Consequently, since the Eighth Amendment forbidding cruel and unusual punishment was prepared by men who accepted English common law, there could be no question that the Eighth Amendment prohibited the execution of the insane.

The issue then became the method the state used to determine Ford's insanity. The High Court noted that Florida did not allow the submission of materials that might be relevant to the decision whether or not to execute the condemned man. In addition, Ford's lawyers were not given the chance to question the state-appointed psychiatrists about the basis for finding their client competent. Questions the defense could have asked included the possibility of personal bias on the doctors' part toward the death penalty, any history of error in their judgment, and their degree of certainty in reaching their conclusions. Finally, the justices pointed out that the greatest defect in Florida's practice is its entrusting the ultimate decision of the execution entirely within the executive branch. The High Court observed,

Under this procedure, the person who appoints the experts and ultimately decides whether the State will be able to carry out the sentence that it has long sought is the Governor, whose subordinates have been responsible for initiating every stage of the prosecution of the condemned from arrest through sentencing. The commander of the State's corps of prosecutors cannot be said to have the neutrality that is necessary for reliability in the fact-finding proceeding.

The High Court further observed that, even though a prisoner has been sentenced to death, he is still protected by the Constitution. Therefore, ascertaining his sanity as a basis for a legal execution is as important as other proceedings in a capital case.

In dissent, Justice Rehnquist, joined by Chief Justice Burger, thought the Florida procedure consistent with English common law, which had left the decision to the executive branch. Rehnquist warned,

A claim of insanity may be made at any time before sentence and, once rejected, may be raised again; a prisoner found sane two days before execution might claim to have lost his sanity the next day, thus necessitating another judicial determination of his sanity and presumably another stay of his execution.

CAN A MENTALLY RETARDED PERSON BE EXECUTED?

Pamela Carpenter was brutally raped, beaten, and stabbed with a pair of scissors. Before she died, she was able to describe her attacker, and as a result, Johnny Penry was arrested for, and later confessed to, the crime. He was found guilty and sentenced to die.

Among the issues considered in his appeal was whether the State of Texas could execute a mentally retarded person. At Penry's competency hear-

ing, a psychiatrist testified that the defendant had an I.Q. of 54. (Penry had been tested in the past as having an IQ between 50 and 63, indicating mild to moderate retardation.) According to the psychiatrist, during the commission of the crime, 22-year-old Penry had the mental age of a child six and one-half years old and the social maturity of a 9- to 10-year-old. Penry's attorneys argued,

Because of their mental disabilities, mentally retarded people do not possess the level of moral culpability (blameworthiness) to justify imposing the death sentence.... [T]here is an emerging national consensus (majority view) against executing the retarded.

Writing for the five-person majority (Justices O'Connor, Rehnquist, White, Scalia, and Kennedy) regarding the execution of mentally retarded persons, Justice O'Connor, in *Penry v. Lynaugh* (492 U.S. 302, 1989), found no emerging national consensus against such execution. Furthermore, while, historically, idiots and profoundly retarded persons had not been executed for murder, Penry did not fall into this group.

Justice O'Connor noted that Penry was found competent to stand trial. He was able to rationally consult with his lawyer and understood the proceedings against him. Justice O'Connor thought that the defense was guilty of lumping all mentally retarded persons together, ascribing, among other things, a lack of moral capacity to be culpable for actions that call for the death punishment.

Mentally retarded persons are individuals whose abilities and experiences can vary greatly.... If the mentally retarded were not treated as individuals, but as an undifferentiated group, a mildly mentally retarded person could be denied the opportunity to enter into contracts or to marry by virtue of the fact that he had a "mental age" of a young child. In light of the diverse capacities and life experiences of mentally retarded persons, it cannot be said on the

36

record before us today that all mentally retarded people, by definition, can never act with the level of culpability associated with the death penalty.

Further, the majority could find no national movement toward any type of consensus on this issue. While *Penry* produced several public opinion polls that indicated strong public opposition to executing the retarded, almost none of this public opinion was reflected in death penalty legislation. Only the federal Anti-Drug Abuse Act of 1988 (PL 100-690) and the State of Georgia banned the execution of retarded persons found guilty of a capital crime.

Justice Brennan disagreed. While he agreed that lumping mentally retarded people together might result in stereotyping and discrimination, there are characteristics that fall under the clinical definition of mental retardation. Citing the *amicus* brief prepared by the American Association on Mental Retardation, Justice Brennan noted,

Every individual who has mental retardation — irrespective of her precise capacities or experiences — has a substantial disability in cognitive ability and adaptive behavior.... Though individuals, particularly those who are mildly retarded, may be quite capable of overcoming these limitations to the extent of being able to "maintain themselves independently or semi-independently in the community," nevertheless, the mentally retarded, by definition, "have a reduced ability to cope with and function in the everyday world."

Justice Brennan did not believe that executing a person not fully responsible for his or her actions would serve the "penal goals of retribution or deterrence." What is the point of executing someone who did not fully recognize the terrible evil that he or she had done? Furthermore, executing a mentally retarded person would not deter nonretarded people, those who would be aware of the possibility of an execution.

COMPETENCY STANDARD

Moran fatally shot a bartender and a patron four times each, and several days later, his former wife. Failing a suicide attempt, Moran confessed to his crime. Later on, the defendant pleaded not guilty to three counts of first-degree murder. Two psychiatrists examined Moran and concluded that he was competent to stand trial. Approximately 10 weeks after the evaluations, the defendant decided to dismiss his attorneys and change his plea to guilty. After review of the psychiatric reports, the trial court accepted the waiver for counsel and the guilty plea. The defendant was later sentenced to death.

Seven months later, Moran appealed his case, claiming that he had been "mentally incompetent to represent himself." The appellate court reversed the conviction, ruling that "competency to waive constitutional rights requires a higher level of mental functioning than that required to stand trial." A defendant is considered competent to stand trial if he can understand the proceedings and help in his defense. On the other hand, for a defendant to be considered competent to waive counsel or to plead guilty, he has to be capable of " 'reasoned choice' among the alternatives available to him." The appellate court found Moran mentally incapable of the reasoned choice needed to be in a position to waive his constitutional rights.

In a 7-2 decision, the Supreme Court, in *Godinez v. Moran* (509 U.S. 389, 1993), reversed the judgment of the court of appeals, holding that the standard for measuring a criminal defendant's competency to plead guilty or to waive his right to counsel is not higher than the standard for standing trial. The High Court then sent the case back to the lower courts for further proceedings.

RACE AS A CONSIDERATION

In 1978, Willie Lloyd Turner, a Black man, robbed a jewelry store in Franklin, Virginia. Angered because the owner had set off a silent alarm, Turner first shot the owner in the head, wounding him, and then shot him twice in the chest, killing him for "snitching." Turner's lawyer included the following question for the jurors:

The defendant, Willie Lloyd Turner, is a member of the Negro race. The victim, W. Jack Smith, Jr., was a white Caucasian. Will these facts prejudice you against Willie Lloyd Turner or affect your ability to render a fair and impartial verdict based solely on the evidence?

The judge refused to allow this question to be asked. A jury of eight Whites and four Blacks convicted Turner and then, in a separate sentencing hearing, recommended the death sentence, which the judge imposed.

Turner appealed his conviction, claiming that the judge's refusal to ask prospective jurors about their racial attitudes deprived him of his right to a fair trial. Although his argument failed to convince state and federal appeals courts, the U.S. Supreme Court heard his case. In *Turner v. Murray* (476 U.S. 28, 1986), the High Court, in a 7-2 decision, overturned Turner's death sentence, but not his conviction.

Writing for the majority, Justice White noted that, in considering a death sentence, the jury makes a subjective decision that is uniquely his or her own regarding what punishment should be meted out to the offender. Justice White further stated,

Because of the range of discretion entrusted to a jury in a capital sentencing hearing, there is a unique opportunity for racial prejudice to operate but remain undetected. On the facts of this case, a juror who believes that blacks are violence-prone or morally inferior might well be influenced by that belief in deciding whether petitioner's crime involved the aggravating factors specified under Virginia law. Such a juror might also be less favorably inclined toward petitioner's evidence of mental disturbance as a mitigating circum-

stance. More subtle, less consciously held racial attitudes could also influence a juror's decision in this case. Fear of blacks, which could easily be stirred up by the violent facts of petitioner's crime, might incline a juror to favor the death penalty.

The High Court recognized the fact that the death sentence differs from all other punishments and, therefore, requires a more comprehensive examination of how it is imposed. The lower court judge, by not asking prospective jurors about their racial attitudes, had not exercised this thorough examination. Consequently, the Supreme Court reversed Turner's death sentence. Justice Powell, in his dissent, observed,

[The Court ruling seemed to be] based on what amounts to a constitutional presumption that jurors in capital cases are racially biased. Such presumption unjustifiably suggests that criminal justice in our courts of law is meted out on racial grounds....

Limits to Consideration of Racial Attitudes

Warren McCleskey and three other armed men robbed a furniture store in Fulton County, Georgia. A police officer, responding to a silent alarm, entered the store, was shot twice, and died. McCleskey was Black; the officer was White. McCleskey admitted taking part in the robbery, but denied shooting the policeman. The state proved that at least one shot came from the weapon McCleskey was carrying and produced two witnesses who had heard McCleskey admit to the shooting. A jury found him guilty and McCleskey, offering no mitigating circumstances during the sentencing phase, received the death penalty.

McCleskey eventually appealed his case all the way to the U.S. Supreme Court. Part of his appeal was based upon two major statistical studies of over 2,000 Georgia murder cases that occurred during the 1970s. Prepared by Professors David C. Baldus, George Woodworth, and Charles Pulanski, the statistical analysis was called the *Baldus Study*.

The *Baldus Study* found that defendants charged with killing White persons received the death penalty in 11 percent of cases, but defendants charged with killing Blacks received the death penalty in only 1 percent of the cases. Interestingly, the study also found a reverse racial difference, based on the defendant's race — 4 percent of the Black defendants received the death penalty, as opposed to 7 percent of the White defendants.

Furthermore, the *Baldus Study* reported on the cases, based on the combination of the defendant's race and that of the victim. The death penalty was imposed in 22 percent of the cases involving Black defendants and White victims, in 8 percent of the cases involving White defendants and White victims, in 3 percent of the cases involving White defendants and Black victims, and in 1 percent of the cases involving Black defendants and Black victims.

The *Baldus Study* also found that prosecutors sought the death penalty in 70 percent of the cases involving Black defendants and White victims, in 32 percent of the cases involving White defendants and White victims, in 19 percent of the cases involving White defendants and Black victims, and in 15 percent of the cases involving Black defendants and Black victims.

Finally, after taking account of variables that could have explained the differences on nonracial grounds, the study concluded that defendants charged with killing White victims were 4.3 times as likely to receive the death penalty as defendants charged with killing Blacks. In addition, Black defendants were 1.1 times as likely to get a death sentence as other defendants were. Therefore, McCleskey, who was Black and killed a White victim, had the greatest likelihood of being sentenced to death.

In court testimony, Dr. Baldus testified that, in really brutal cases where there is no question the death penalty should be imposed, racial discrimination on the part of the jurors tends to disappear. The racial factors usually come into play in mid-range cases, such as McCleskey's, where the jurors were faced with choices.

While the federal district court did not accept the *Baldus Study*, both the court of appeals and the U.S. Supreme Court accepted the study as valid. However, a 5-4 Supreme Court, in *McCleskey v. Kemp* (481 U.S. 279, 1987), rejected McCleskey's appeal. McCleskey had to show that the state of Georgia had acted in a discriminatory manner in his case, and the *Baldus Study* was not enough to support the defendant's claim that any of the jurors had acted with discrimination.

Judge Powell noted that statistics, at most, may show that a certain factor might likely enter some decision-making processes. The Court recognized that jury decision could be influenced by racial prejudice, but the majority believed previous rulings had built in enough safeguards to guarantee equal protection for every defendant. The Court declared,

> At most, the *Baldus Study* indicates a discrepancy that appears to correlate with race. Apparent disparities in sentencing are an inevitable part of our criminal justice system.... Where the discretion that is fundamental to our criminal process is involved, we decline to assume that what is unexplained is invidious (unfairly discriminatory).... [W]e hold that the *Baldus Study* does not demonstrate a constitutionally significant risk of racial bias affecting the Georgia capital-sentencing process.

The Court expressed concern that if they found that Baldus' findings did represent a risk, it might well be applied to lesser cases. It further noted that it is the job of the legislative branch to consider these findings and incorporate them into the laws to guarantee equal protection in courts of law.

Justice Brennan, who, along with Justice Marshall, believed capital punishment constitutes cruel and unusual punishment and, therefore, unconstitutional, thought the *Baldus Study* powerfully showed that it is impossible to eliminate arbitrariness in the imposition of the death penalty. Therefore, it must be abolished altogether because the Court cannot rely on legal safeguards to guarantee a Black defendant a fair sentencing. While the *Baldus Study* did not show that racism necessarily led to McCleskey's death sentence, it had surely shown that McCleskey faced a considerably greater likelihood of being sentenced to death because he was a Black man convicted of killing a White man.

Also writing in dissent, Justice Blackmun thought the Court majority had concentrated too much on the potential racial attitudes of the jury. As important, he thought, were the racial attitudes of the prosecutor's office, which the *Baldus Study* found to be much more likely to seek the death penalty for a Black who had killed a White than other categories.

The district attorney for Fulton County had testified that no county policy existed on how to prosecute capital cases. Decisions to seek the death penalty were left to the judgment of the assistant district attorneys who handled the cases. Blackmun thought that such a system was certainly open to abuse. Without guidelines, the prosecutors could let their racial prejudices influence their decisions.

Blackmun also noted that the court majority had totally dismissed Georgia's history of racial prejudice as past history. While it should not be the overriding factor, it should be considered in any case presented to the High Court. Justice Blackmun found most disturbing the Court's concern that, if the Baldus findings were upheld, they might be applied to other cases, leading to constitutional challenges. Blackmun thought that a closer scrutiny of the effects of racial discrimination would benefit the criminal justice system and, ultimately, society.

The Race of Jurors and Equal Protection

James A. Ford, a Black man, was charged with the kidnapping, rape, and murder of a White woman. The state informed Ford that it planned to seek the death penalty. Before the trial, Ford filed a "Motion to Restrict Racial Use of Peremptory Challenges," claiming that the prosecutor had consistently excluded Black persons from juries where the victim was White.

At a hearing on the defendant's motion, Ford's lawyer noted that it had been his experience that the district attorney and his assistants had used their peremptory challenges (the right to reject a juror without giving a reason) to excuse potential Black jurors. Ford's lawyer asked the trial judge to prevent this by ordering the district attorney to justify on the record his reasons for excusing potential Black jurors.

The prosecutor denied any discrimination on his part. He referred to the U.S. Supreme Court decision in *Swain v. Alabama* (380 U.S. 202, 1965), which said, in part, "It would be an unreasonable burden to require an attorney for either side to justify his use of peremptory challenges." The judge denied Ford's attorney's motion because he had previously seen the district attorney passing over prospective White jurors in favor of potential Black jurors.

During jury selection, the prosecutor used nine of his 10 peremptory challenges to dismiss prospective Black jurors, leaving only one Black member seated on the jury. In closed sessions, the judge allowed Ford's attorney's observation, for the record, that nine of the 10 Black prospective members had been dismissed on peremptory challenges by the prosecutor. However, the judge told the prosecutor that he did not have to offer any reasons for his peremptory actions.

Ford was convicted on all counts and was sentenced to death. His attorney called for a new trial and claimed that Ford's "right to an impartial jury as guaranteed by the Sixth Amendment (calling for a fair cross-section of the community) of the United States Constitution was violated by the prosecutor's exercise of his peremptory challenges on a racial basis." On appeal, the Supreme Court of Georgia affirmed the conviction.

Ford appealed to the U.S. Supreme Court. In *Ford v. Georgia* (498 U.S. 411, 1991), the High Court reversed the decision of the Georgia Supreme Court. The Court vacated (annulled) Ford's conviction and ruled that its decision on *Batson v. Kentucky* (476 U.S. 79) could be applied retroactively to Ford's case. In 1986, the High Court had ruled in *Batson*, which dropped the *Swain* requirement of proof of prior discrimination, that a Black defendant could make a case, claiming the denial of equal protection of the laws. The defendant could do so solely on evidence that the prosecutor had used peremptory challenges to exclude members of the defendant's race from the jury.

Delivering the opinion for a unanimous Court, Justice Souter held that the Georgia Supreme Court had erred when it ruled that Ford had failed to present a proper equal protection claim. Although Ford's pretrial motion did not mention the Equal Protection Clause (of the Fourteenth Amendment), and his new trial motion had cited the Sixth Amendment rather than the Fourteenth, the motion referring to a pattern of excluding Black members "over a long period of time asserts an equal protection claim."

METHODS OF EXECUTION

Lethal Injection May Be Used for Executions

The injection of a deadly combination of drugs has become the method of execution in most states permitting capital punishment. Condemned prisoners from Texas and Oklahoma, two of the first states to introduce this method, brought suit claiming that, while the drugs used had been approved by the Food and Drug Administration (FDA) for medical purposes, they had never been approved for use in nor tested for human executions.

The petitioners further claimed that, since the drugs would likely be administered by untrained personnel, they might not cause the quick and painless death intended. They alleged these drugs had been "misbranded," a violation of 21 U.S.C. para. 352 (f), which states, "A drug or device shall be

deemed to be misbranded ... [u]nless its labeling bears (1) adequate directions for use...." In addition, since the drugs were being put to a new use, they had to be reapproved by the FDA to determine if they were "safe and effective" for human execution.

The FDA Commissioner refused to act, claiming serious questions as to whether the agency had jurisdiction in the area. He further noted,

Generally, enforcement proceedings in this area are initiated only when there is a serious danger to the public health or a blatant scheme to defraud. We cannot conclude that those dangers are present under State lethal injections laws, which are duly authorized statutory enactments in furtherance of proper State [goals].

The U.S. District Court for the District of Columbia disagreed with the condemned prisoners that the FDA had a responsibility to determine if the lethal mixture used during execution was safe and effective. The court noted that decisions by a federal agency not to take action were not reviewable in court.

A divided Court of Appeals for the District of Columbia reversed the lower court ruling, noting that the FDA's own policy required the FDA to investigate the unapproved use of an approved drug when such use became "widespread" or "endanger[ed] the public health." Therefore, the prisoners who risked a "cruel and protracted" death were entitled to a more thorough investigation of the drugs used in their execution.

A generally irritated U.S. Supreme Court agreed to hear the case "to review the implausible result that the FDA is required to exercise its enforcement power to ensure that States use only drugs that are 'safe and effective' for human execution."

In *Heckler v. Chaney* (470 U.S. 821, 1985), the unanimous Court agreed that, in this case, the

FDA did not have jurisdiction, although Justices Brennan and Marshall indicated that the limitation on court jurisdiction should not apply to all agency decisions not to intervene. The remaining justices, on the other hand, thought the courts had no right to question any agency decision not to take action.

Writing for all but Justices Marshall and Brennan, Justice Rehnquist explained why the majority of justices concluded that the FDA decision not to investigate the prisoner's request was simply not the High Court's business.

First, an agency decision not to enforce often involves a complicated balancing of a number of factors which are peculiarly within its expertise. Thus, the agency must not only assess where a violation has occurred, but whether agency resources are best spent on this violation or another, whether the agency is likely to succeed if it acts, whether the particular enforcement action requested best fits the agency's overall policies, and indeed, whether the agency has enough resources to undertake the action at all. An agency generally cannot act against each technical violation of the statute it is charged with enforcing. The agency is better equipped than the courts to deal with the many variables involved in the proper ordering of its priorities.

Are Executions by
Hanging and Lethal Gas Constitutional?

Hanging

Washington state law imposes capital punishment either by "hanging by the neck" or, if the condemned chooses, by lethal injection. Charles Rodham Campbell was convicted of three counts of murder in 1982 and sentenced to death. Campbell, in challenging the constitutionality of hanging under the Washington statute, claimed that execution by hanging violated his Eighth Amendment right because it was cruel and unusual punishment. Furthermore, the direction that he be

hanged unless he chose lethal injection was cruel and unusual punishment. He claimed that such instruction further violated his First Amendment right by forcing him to participate in his own execution to avoid hanging.

In *Campbell v. Wood* (18 F.3d. 662, 9th Cir. 1994), the U.S. Court of Appeals for the Ninth Circuit noted,

We do not consider hanging to be cruel and unusual simply because it causes death, or because there may be some pain associated with death.... As used in the Constitution, "cruel" implies "something inhuman and barbarous, something more than the mere extinguishment of life."... Campbell is entitled to an execution free only of "the unnecessary and wanton infliction of pain."

According to the Court, just because the defendant was given a choice of a method of execution did not mean that he was being subjected to cruel and unusual punishment.

We believe that benefits to prisoners who may choose to exercise the option and who may feel relieved that they can elect lethal injection outweigh the emotional costs to those who find the mere existence of an option objectionable.

Campbell argued that the state was infringing on his First Amendment right of free exercise of his religion. He claimed that it was against his religion to participate in his own execution by being allowed to elect lethal injection over hanging.

The Court contended that Campbell did not have to choose an execution method or participate in his own execution. "He may remain absolutely silent and refuse to participate in any election." The death penalty statute does not require him to choose the method of execution; it simply offers a choice. Upon appeal (*Campbell v. Wood*, 511 U.S. 1119, 1994), the U.S. Supreme Court decided not to hear the case.

Lethal Gas

In April 1992, three California death row inmates (David Fierro, Alejandro Ruiz, and Robert Harris) filed a suit on behalf of themselves and all others under sentence of execution by lethal gas. The inmates alleged that California's method of execution by lethal gas violated the Eighth and Fourteenth Amendments.

In October 1994, a federal district judge, Marilyn Hall Patel, ruled that execution by lethal gas "is inhumane and has no place in civilized society." She then ordered California's gas chamber closed and that lethal injection be used instead. This was the first time a federal judge had ruled that any method of execution violated the Eighth and Fourteenth Amendment.

While the state of California maintained that cyanide gas caused almost instant unconsciousness, the judge referred to doctors' reports and witnesses' accounts of gas chamber executions, which indicated that the dying inmates stayed conscious for 15 seconds to a minute or longer and suffered "intense physical pain." In 1993, the California legislature amended its death statute, providing that, if lethal gas "is held invalid, the punishment of death shall be imposed by the alternative means," lethal injection.

James Gomez, director of the California Department of Corrections, and Arthur Calderon, warden of San Quentin Prison, appealed. In February 1996, in *Fierro v. Gomez* (77 F.3d 301, 9th Cir.), the U.S. Court of Appeals for the Ninth Circuit affirmed the rulings of the federal district court.

Gomez appealed the case to the U.S. Supreme Court. In October 1996, the 7-2 Supreme Court, in *Gomez v. Fierro* (65 LW 3291), vacated (annulled) the appellate court's ruling and returned the case to the appellate court for additional proceedings, citing the newly amended death penalty statute (lethal injection as an alternative to lethal gas; see above).

CHAPTER V

DEATH PENALTY STATUTES AND METHODS

CAPITAL OFFENSES

Most death penalty statutes in force prior to the *Furman v. Georgia* (408 U.S. 238) decision of June 29, 1972, provided for the imposition of the death penalty for capital murder and, in some states, for other crimes. However, in *Furman*, the U.S. Supreme Court found that the death penalty, as then being administered, was "cruel and unusual punishment" in violation of the Eighth Amendment of the U.S. Constitution (see Chapter II). Many states revised their laws to conform to standards set by the *Furman* decision. Since *Furman*, review of individual state statutes has continued as appeals of capital sentences reach state courts or the U.S. Supreme Court.

Under revised state laws, different types of capital murder have been specifically defined. Although varying somewhat from one jurisdiction to another, the types of homicide most commonly specified are murder carried out during the commission of a felony; murder of a peace officer, corrections employee, or fireman engaged in the performance of official duties; murder by an inmate serving a life sentence; and murder for hire (contract murder). Different statutory terminology may be used by different states to designate basically identical crimes. In some states, such terms as "murder," "first-degree murder," or "murder Class A felony" may indicate the same capital offense. At yearend 1998, the death penalty was authorized by the statutes of 38 states (Table 5.1) and by the federal government (Table 5.2).

While other offenses (most notably, treason and air piracy, or hijacking) also carry the death penalty, most have not yet had their constitutionality tested. The Supreme Court has held, in *Everheart v. Georgia* (433 U.S. 917, 1977) and *Coker v. Georgia* (433 U.S. 584, 1977), that rape and kidnapping, as horrible as they are, do not result in death, and, therefore, do not warrant the death penalty (see Chapter III). Nonetheless, in 1995, the Louisiana legislature amended statute La. R.S. 14:42(C) to allow for the death penalty when the victim of rape is less than 12 years old (see below).

RECENT STATUTORY CHANGES

In 1998, no state enacted new legislation authorizing capital punishment. As in the past, states continued to revise their statutory provisions relating to the death penalty. In 1998, most statutory changes involved aggravating (adding to the gravity of a crime) or mitigating (lessening the gravity of a crime) circumstances, procedural amendments, and revisions to capital offenses.

In 1998, 13 states revised their laws that related to the death penalty. Among changes made, three states (Kentucky, Tennessee, and Mississippi) authorized lethal injection as a method of execution. In Kentucky, the offender sentenced to death on or after March 31, 1998, could choose between lethal injection and electrocution. In Tennessee, a person on death row whose offense occurred on or before January 1, 1999, could choose lethal injection by requesting in writing a waiver of the method used at the time of his or her offense. Mississippi replaced execution by lethal gas with lethal injection.

The Kentucky legislature also passed the Kentucky Racial Justice Act (SB 171), which prohibits the execution of a person when evidence shows racial bias in prosecution or sentencing. The legislature further set procedures to handle claims made under this law.

Aside from authorizing lethal injection as a method of execution, Mississippi revised its statute by eliminating capital rape. The statute that imposed the death penalty for the rape of a child under age 14 by a person 18 or older was rewritten as a statutory-rape provision that is not punishable by death. In addition, executions, previously held at midnight, would now take place at 6 p.m. or within 24 hours of the time for which the death warrant has been signed. The amended statute allows two members of the victim's family to be present at the execution.

Besides replacing electrocution with lethal injection as the execution method, Tennessee extended its definition of felony murder to include aggravated child neglect.

TABLE 5.1

Capital offenses, by State, 1998

Alabama. Capital murder with a finding of at least 1 of 9 aggravating circumstances (Ala. Code § 13A-5-40 and § 13A-5-49).

Arizona. First-degree murder accompanied by at least 1 of 10 aggravating factors.

Arkansas. Capital murder (Ark. Code Ann. 5-10-101) with a finding of at least 1 of 10 aggravating circumstances; treason.

California. First-degree murder with special circumstances; train wrecking; treason; perjury causing execution.

Colorado. First-degree murder with at least 1 of 13 aggravating factors; treason. Capital sentencing excludes persons determined to be mentally retarded.

Connecticut. Capital felony with 9 categories of aggravated homicide (C.G.S. 53a-54b).

Delaware. First-degree murder with aggravating circumstances.

Florida. First-degree murder; felony murder; capital drug trafficking.

Georgia. Murder; kidnaping with bodily injury or ransom where the victim dies; aircraft hijacking; treason.

Idaho. First-degree murder; aggravated kidnaping.

Illinois. First-degree murder with 1 of 15 aggravating circumstances.

Indiana. Murder with 16 aggravating circumstances (IC 35-50-2-9). Capital sentencing excludes persons determined to be mentally retarded.

Kansas. Capital murder with 7 aggravating circumstances (KSA 21-3439). Capital sentencing excludes persons determined to be mentally retarded.

Kentucky. Murder with aggravating factors; kidnaping with aggravating factors.

Louisiana. First-degree murder; aggravated rape of victim under age 12; treason (La. R.S. 14:30, 14:42, and 14:113).

Maryland. First-degree murder, either premeditated or during the commission of a felony, provided that certain death eligibility requirements are satisfied.

Mississippi. Capital murder (97-3-19(2) MCA); aircraft piracy (97-25-55(1) MCA).

Missouri. First-degree murder (565.020 RSMO).

Montana. Capital murder with 1 of 9 aggravating circumstances (46-18-303 MCA); capital sexual assault (45-5-503 MCA).

Nebraska. First-degree murder with a finding of at least 1 statutorily-defined aggravating circumstance.

Nevada. First-degree murder with 13 aggravating circumstances.

New Hampshire. Six categories of capital murder (RSA 630:1 and RSA 630:5).

New Jersey. Purposeful or knowing murder by one's own conduct; contract murder; solicitation by command or threat in furtherance of a narcotics conspiracy (NJSA 2C:11-3C).

New Mexico. First-degree murder in conjunction with a finding of at least 1 of 7 aggravating circumstances (Section 30-2-1 A, NMSA).

New York. First-degree murder with 1 of 12 aggravating factors. Capital sentencing excludes persons determined to be mentally retarded.

North Carolina. First-degree murder (N.C.G.S. 14-17).

Ohio. Aggravated murder with at least 1 of 8 aggravating circumstances. (O.R.C. secs. 2903.01, 2929.01, and 2929.04).

Oklahoma. First-degree murder in conjunction with a finding of at least 1 of 8 statutorily defined aggravating circumstances.

Oregon. Aggravated murder (ORS 163.095).

Pennsylvania. First-degree murder with 18 aggravating circumstances.

South Carolina. Murder with 1 of 10 aggravating circumstances (§ 16-3-20(C)(a)). Mental retardation is a mitigating factor.

South Dakota. First-degree murder with 1 of 10 aggravating circumstances; aggravated kidnaping.

Tennessee. First-degree murder.

Texas. Criminal homicide with 1 of 8 aggravating circumstances (TX Penal Code 19.03).

Utah. Aggravated murder (76-5-202, Utah Code annotated).

Virginia. First-degree murder with 1 of 12 aggravating circumstances (VA Code § 18.2-31).

Washington. Aggravated first-degree murder.

Wyoming. First-degree murder.

Source: Tracy L. Snell, *Capital Punishment 1998*, Bureau of Justice Statistics, Washington, DC, 1999

TABLE 5.2

Federal laws providing for the death penalty, 1998

8 U.S.C. 1342 — Murder related to the smuggling of aliens.

18 U.S.C. 32-34 — Destruction of aircraft, motor vehicles, or related facilities resulting in death.

18 U.S.C. 36 — Murder committed during a drug-related drive-by shooting.

18 U.S.C. 37 — Murder committed at an airport serving international civil aviation.

18 U.S.C. 115(b)(3) [by cross-reference to 18 U.S.C. 1111] — Retaliatory murder of a member of the immediate family of law enforcement officials.

18 U.S.C. 241, 242, 245, 247 — Civil rights offenses resulting in death.

18 U.S.C. 351 [by cross-reference to 18 U.S.C. 1111] — Murder of a member of Congress, an important executive official, or a Supreme Court Justice.

18 U.S.C. 794 — Espionage.

18 U.S.C. 844(d), (f), (i) — Death resulting from offenses involving transportation of explosives, destruction of government property, or destruction of property related to foreign or interstate commerce.

18 U.S.C. 924(i) — Murder committed by the use of a firearm during a crime of violence or a drug-trafficking crime.

18 U.S.C. 930 — Murder committed in a Federal Government facility.

18 U.S.C. 1091 — Genocide.

18 U.S.C. 1111 — First-degree murder.

18 U.S.C. 1114 — Murder of a Federal judge or law enforcement official.

18 U.S.C. 1116 — Murder of a foreign official.

18 U.S.C. 1118 — Murder by a Federal prisoner.

18 U.S.C. 1119 — Murder of a U.S. national in a foreign country.

18 U.S.C. 1120 — Murder by an escaped Federal prisoner already sentenced to life imprisonment.

18 U.S.C. 1121 — Murder of a State or local law enforcement official or other person aiding in a Federal investigation; murder of a State correctional officer.

18 U.S.C. 1201 — Murder during a kidnaping.

18 U.S.C. 1203 — Murder during a hostage taking.

18 U.S.C. 1503 — Murder of a court officer or juror.

18 U.S.C. 1512 — Murder with the intent of preventing testimony by a witness, victim, or informant.

18 U.S.C. 1513 — Retaliatory murder of a witness, victim, or informant.

18 U.S.C. 1716 — Mailing of injurious articles with intent to kill or resulting in death.

18 U.S.C. 1751 [by cross-reference to 18 U.S.C. 1111] — Assassination or kidnaping resulting in the death of the President or Vice President.

18 U.S.C. 1958 — Murder for hire.

18 U.S.C. 1959 — Murder involved in a racketeering offense.

18 U.S.C. 1992 — Willful wrecking of a train resulting in death.

18 U.S.C. 2113 — Bank-robbery-related murder or kidnaping.

18 U.S.C. 2119 — Murder related to a carjacking.

18 U.S.C. 2245 — Murder related to rape or child molestation.

18 U.S.C. 2251 — Murder related to sexual exploitation of children.

18 U.S.C. 2280 — Murder committed during an offense against maritime navigation.

18 U.S.C. 2281 — Murder committed during an offense against a maritime fixed platform.

18 U.S.C. 2332 — Terrorist murder of a U.S. national in another country.

18 U.S.C. 2332a — Murder by the use of a weapon of mass destruction.

18 U.S.C. 2340 — Murder involving torture.

18 U.S.C. 2381 — Treason.

21 U.S.C. 848(e) — Murder related to a continuing criminal enterprise or related murder of a Federal, State, or local law enforcement officer.

49 U.S.C. 1472-1473 — Death resulting from aircraft hijacking.

Source: Tracy L. Snell, *Capital Punishment 1998*, Bureau of Justice Statistics, Washington, DC, 1999

The state further revised its death penalty statute to allow victim impact statements (see Chapter III) and the introduction of facts and circumstances of a defendant's prior criminal history of violence.

To its death penalty law, Washington added as aggravating factors the murder of a person who had a protective order against the defendant and the murder of a person the defendant lived with when the defendant had previously assaulted or harassed the victim three or more times. Indiana's criminal code added as an aggravating factor the murder of a pregnant woman. Ohio revised the procedure for vacating (annulling) a death sentence against a person who was under 18 at the commission of the crime and for suspending the execution of a pregnant or insane offender.

RECENT CHALLENGES TO STATE DEATH PENALTY LAWS

Louisiana

On December 13, 1996, the Louisiana Supreme Court, in *Louisiana v. Wilson* (1996 WL 718217), held that the state death penalty statute was constitutional. Two defendants charged with raping young girls moved to quash their indictments. They claimed that the death penalty, when imposed for rape, constitutes "cruel and unusual punishment" and, therefore, is unconstitutional under the Eighth Amendment and Article I, § 20 of the Louisiana Constitution.

Anthony Wilson was charged by a grand jury with the aggravated rape of a five-year-old girl. Patrick Dwayne Bethley was charged with raping three girls, one of whom was his daughter. At the time of the rape, the girls were five, seven, and nine years old. The Louisiana Supreme Court concluded,

> ... [G]iven the appalling nature of the crime, the severity of the harm inflicted upon the victim, and the harm imposed on society, the death penalty is not an excessive penalty for the crime of rape when the victim is a child under the age of twelve years old.

New York

New York's death penalty statute prohibited the imposition of a death sentence where a defendant enters a guilty plea, while a defendant pleading not guilty would have to stand trial and face the possibility of a death sentence. The maximum penalty in the first case would be life imprisonment without parole. In other words, the law provided two levels of penalty for the same offense, imposing the death penalty only on those who claimed innocence.

Defendants in two capital cases challenged the plea provisions of New York's death penalty statute, claiming these provisions violated their Fifth Amendment right against self-incrimination and Sixth Amendment right to a jury trial. On December 22, 1998, the New York Court of Appeals, in *Hynes v. Tomei* (including *Relin v. Mateo*, 92 N.Y.2d 613, 706 N.E.2d 1201, 684 N.Y.S.2d 177), unanimously agreed, striking down these plea-bargaining provisions as unconstitutional. The court, relying on the U.S. Supreme Court decision in *United States v. Jackson* (390 U.S. 570, 1968), observed that "the Supreme Court in *Jackson* prohibited statutes that 'needlessly' encourage guilty pleas, which are not constitutionally protected, by impermissibly burdening constitutional rights."

MINIMUM AGE FOR EXECUTION

The first execution of a juvenile, Thomas Graunger, occurred in 1642 in Plymouth Colony, Massachusetts. The United States has since executed an estimated 356 persons (as of 1999) who were juveniles during the commission of the crime. Between the reinstatement of the death penalty in 1976 and December 31, 1999, 13 inmates who were juveniles at the time of their crimes were executed. For 2000, the United States had scheduled the execution of five death row inmates who were all 17

TABLE 5.3

Minimum age authorized for capital punishment, 1998

Age 16 or less	Age 17	Age 18	None specified
Alabama (16)	Georgia	California	Arizona
Arkansas (14)ᵃ	New Hampshire	Colorado	Idaho
Delaware (16)	North Carolinaᵇ	Connecticutᶜ	Louisiana
Florida (16)	Texas	Federal system	Montana
Indiana (16)		Illinois	Pennsylvania
Kentucky (16)		Kansas	South Carolina
Mississippi (16)ᵈ		Maryland	South Dakotaᵉ
Missouri (16)		Nebraska	Utah
Nevada (16)		New Jersey	
Oklahoma (16)		New Mexico	
Virginia (14)ᶠ		New York	
Wyoming (16)		Ohio	
		Oregon	
		Tennessee	
		Washington	

Note: Reporting by States reflects interpretations by State attorney generals' offices and may differ from previously reported ages.
ᵃSee Ark. Code Ann. 9-27-318(b)(2)(Repl. 1991).
ᵇAge required is 17 unless the murderer was incarcerated for murder when a subsequent murder occurred; then the age may be 14.
ᶜSee Conn. Gen. Stat. 53a-46a(g)(1).
ᵈThe minimum age defined by statute is 13, but the effective age is 16 based on interpretation of U.S. Supreme Court decisions by the Mississippi Supreme Court.
ᵉJuveniles may be transferred to adult court. Age can be a mitigating factor.
ᶠThe minimum age for transfer to adult court by statute is 14, but the effective age is 16 based on interpretation of U.S. Supreme Court decisions by the State attorney general's office.

Source: Tracy L. Snell, *Capital Punishment 1998*, Bureau of Justice Statistics, Washington, DC, 1999

years old at the commission of the crime. As of January 25, 2000, three had been put to death. Douglas Christopher Thomas (Virginia), Steve Roach (Virginia), and Glen McGinnis (Texas) were ages 26, 23, and 27, respectively, at the time of their deaths. (See also Chapter IX.)

The International Covenant on Civil and Political Rights, the United Nations Convention on the Rights of the Child, and the American Convention on Human Rights (see Chapter IX) forbid the imposition of the death penalty on offenders who committed their crimes under age 18. Although the United States ratified (approved) the International Covenant on Civil and Political Rights, it has reserved the right to execute juveniles. The United States is the only ratifying country that has reserved this right. The United States has signed but not ratified the latter two agreements.

In 1998, only eight states did not specify a minimum age for which the death penalty may be imposed. Fourteen states and the federal government required a minimum age of 18, four states authorized a minimum age of 17, and 12 states required an age of eligibility between 14 and 16. (See Table 5.3.) In some states the minimum age is determined by state laws that define the age at which a juvenile may be transferred to the criminal court for trial as an adult. Once a minor is tried as an adult, he or she could then face the same penalties (including death) to which an adult may be sentenced. The Supreme Court, in *Stanford v. Kentucky* and *Wilkins v. Missouri* (492 U.S. 361, 1989), ruled that a minor as young as 16 years old may be executed (see Chapter IV).

In February 1999, for the first time in 40 years, the United States executed an offender who was 16 during the commission of the crime. Sean Sellers of Oklahoma was 29 years old at the time of execution. He was convicted for the murders of his mother, stepfather, and a convenience-store clerk. His supporters claimed Sellers suffered from multiple personality disorder, which was diagnosed after his conviction. The last time a 16-year-old was executed in the United States was in 1959,

when Maryland executed Leonard Shockley. (See Chapter VII for information about the death row inmates sentenced as juveniles.)

EXECUTING MENTALLY RETARDED PERSONS

According to the Death Penalty Information Center (Washington, DC), which opposes the death penalty, as of January 2000, 34 mentally retarded offenders have been executed since 1976. In 1988, Georgia became the first state to prohibit the execution of murderers found "guilty but mentally retarded." The legislation resulted from the 1986 execution of Jerome Bowden, who had an I.Q. of 65 (normal I.Q. is considered 90 and above).

The federal government and 12 states — Arkansas, Colorado, Georgia, Indiana, Kansas, Kentucky, Maryland, Nebraska, New Mexico, New York (except for murder by a prisoner), Tennessee, and Washington — forbid the execution of mentally retarded offenders. In addition, South Carolina allows mental retardation to be used as a mitigating factor in deciding punishment for murder (Table 5.1).

The federal government, in the Anti-Drug Abuse Act of 1988 (PL 100-690), permits the death penalty for any person working "in furtherance of a continuing criminal enterprise or any person engaging in a drug-related felony offense, who intentionally kills or counsels, commands, or causes the intentional killing of an individual," but forbids the imposition of the death penalty against anyone who is mentally retarded who commits this particular crime.

DEATH PENALTY METHODS

The Eighth Amendment of the United States Bill of Rights, using the language of the English Bill of Rights of 1689, prohibits the use of "cruel and unusual punishment" in carrying out an execution. Although one person was pressed to death (placed between two hard surfaces, eventually dying from the pressure) during the Salem witchcraft trials and some rebellious Blacks were burned at the stake during the early 1700s, these were exceptional cases.

For the most part, neither the colonies nor the United States ever used excessive methods of execution, such as drawing and quartering, burying alive, boiling in oil, sawing in half, or crucifixion. Throughout most of the nineteenth century, civilians sentenced to death were hanged, while the military usually shot spies, traitors, and deserters.

The federal government authorizes the method of execution under two different laws. Crimes prosecuted under 28 CFR, Part 26, call for execution by lethal injection, while offenses covered by the Violent Crime Control and Law Enforcement Act of 1994 (PL 103-322, also known as the Federal Death Penalty Act of 1994) are referred to the state where the conviction occurred. In 1998, 17 states authorized more than one method of execution — lethal injection and an alternative method — generally letting the condemned prisoner choose. However, 5 of these 17 states specified which method must be used, depending on the date of sentencing. (See Table 5.4.)

In 1998, only Delaware, New Hampshire, and Washington authorized the use of the gallows to hang the condemned (Table 5.4). However, the condemned person was given the alternative of death by lethal injection. Washington hanged two murderers in 1993 and 1994, while Delaware hanged a prisoner in January 1996. It was Delaware's first hanging in 50 years and the nation's third since 1965.

Idaho, Oklahoma, and Utah authorized the firing squad method if the condemned prisoner refused lethal injection. However, Oklahoma, concerned about legal challenges to its method of execution, could resort to electrocution if lethal injection was ruled unconstitutional and to the firing squad method if both lethal injection and electrocution were deemed unconstitutional. In January 1996, Utah executed its first prisoner by firing squad, two decades after Gary Gilmore asked the state of Utah to carry out his execution in 1977.

Electrocution

At the end of the nineteenth century, alternating current (AC) electricity became one of the dominant symbols of progress. Many people thought this modern convenience would provide a more humane method of execution. In 1893, the first condemned man was put to death in a crude electric chair. In 1998, 11 states authorized electrocution as the method of execution (Table 5.4). In January 2000, the Florida legislature replaced electrocution with lethal injection as the state's primary execution method (see below).

Does Electrocution Constitute a Cruel and Unusual Punishment?

In the 1900s, although Florida had three botched executions using the electric chair, the state supreme court ruled each time that electrocution does not constitute cruel or unusual punishment. In 1990 and 1997, flames shot out from the headpiece worn by the condemned man. On July 8, 1999, Allen Lee Davis developed a nosebleed.

Thomas Provenzano, scheduled to be electrocuted after Davis, challenged the use of the electric chair as Florida's sole method of execution. In *Provenzano v. Moore* (No. 95,973, September 24, 1999), the Florida Supreme Court, in a 4-3 decision, ruled that the electric chair was not cruel and unusual punishment. The court further reported that Allen Lee Davis's nosebleed occurred prior to the execution and did not result from the electrocution.

Subsequently, the court, as it routinely does with all its rulings, posted the *Provenzano* decision on the Internet. Part of the decision were three photographs of Allen Lee Davis, covered with blood. The photographs, part of Justice Leander Shaw's dissenting opinion, brought public outcry worldwide. Justice Shaw claimed that Davis was "brutally tortured to death."

In October 1999, for the first time, the U.S. Supreme Court agreed to consider the constitutionality of electrocution. Death row inmate Anthony

Braden Bryan asked the U.S. Supreme Court to review his case, based on the unreliability of the electric chair. However, before the High Court could hear the case, the Florida legislature, in a special session, voted to replace electrocution with lethal injection as the primary method of execution. A condemned person, however, may choose the electric chair.

On January 24, 2000, the Supreme Court dismissed *Bryan v. Moore* (No. 99-6723) as moot or irrelevant, based on Florida's new legislation. Governor Jeb Bush agreed to sign the bill in conjunction with a second bill that limits, in most cases, death row inmates to two appeals in state courts, with the second appeal to be filed within six months of the first. This provision cut in half the time limit for the second appeal. As of January 2000, just three states — Alabama, Georgia, and Nebraska — used electrocution as the only method of execution.

Lethal Gas

In 1921, the Nevada legislature authorized the use of lethal gas for capital punishment. The actual law called for the condemned person to be executed in his cell, without warning, while asleep. Prison officials, unable to figure out a practical way to carry out the execution, ended up constructing a gas chamber. In 1924, cyanide gas was used for the first time to execute a condemned man. In 1998, five states authorized the use of lethal gas (Table 5.4). In 1994, a federal judge in California ruled that lethal gas was an inhumane method of execution (see Chapter IV).

Lethal Injection

Over the past several years, most states have adopted lethal injection as a more humane alternative to other methods of execution. Following several legal challenges, the Supreme Court, in *Heckler v. Chaney* (470 U.S. 821, 1985), upheld the use of lethal drug injection (see Chapter IV). As of December 31, 1998, 34 states authorized lethal injection, either solely or as an alternative to another method (Table 5.4).

PUBLIC AND PRIVATE EXECUTIONS

Early arguments for capital punishment centered around the issue of deterrence — that the thought of the death penalty might dissuade a person from committing a crime. Executions used to be held in public as a warning to others. Many executions were conducted in a circus atmosphere, leading to opposition to such a public display. In 1830, the state of New York recommended that executions be done in private, although the decision was left to the local sheriff. Five years later, however, the state legislature passed a law prohibiting all public executions.

The idea of private executions did not catch on quickly. Even when executions were confined to jail courtyards, it was often not difficult to find a perch from which to watch the hanging. By the end of the 1800s, private executions had become the norm, although many public executions still took place. In 1936 a Black man was hanged before a crowd of 20,000 in Owensboro, Kentucky. Many people found the holiday atmosphere, recorded on wire service photographs, so abhorrent that the Kentucky legislature banned public executions two years later. The last public hanging occurred in 1937 in Galena, Missouri, before 500 spectators.

Today some opponents of capital punishment support the idea of public executions. They feel that private executions hide the acts from the public, making them more acceptable. Others have recommended televised executions. On the other hand, some proponents of the death penalty support public executions in the hope that they might act as deterrents to future murderers.

Today, most states limit the number of witnesses present at an execution. Witnesses usually include prison officials, reporters, the victim's family, and the condemned's family and friends. However, in celebrated cases such as that of the Rosenbergs, the convicted spies (1953), and that of the notorious California killer Caryl Chessman (1960), the audience, including numerous reporters, grew to several dozen.

Timothy McVeigh's death sentence in June 1997 for the Oklahoma City bombing has raised the question of how the prison facility would accommodate the hundreds of victims' relatives who would wish to witness the execution. One possibility is the use of closed-circuit television like the one used during the trial, because the courtroom was not big enough for the numerous spectators.

Victim's Family as Witnesses

As of December 1998 (latest data available), the laws of 12 states — Alabama, Arkansas, California, Delaware, Kentucky, Louisiana, Nevada, Ohio, Oklahoma, South Carolina, Tennessee, and Washington — allowed victims' families to be present at executions. The National Center for Victims of Crime reports that the statutes of the different states vary in their procedural requirements, which victims' relatives have to follow in order to request notification and/or attendance.

For example, the Nevada statute defines immediate family as those "... who are related by blood, adoption or marriage, within the second degree of consanguinity (blood relationship) or affinity (relationship by marriage or adoption rather than by blood)." The victim's relatives may write the director of the prison department if they wish notification of the execution. Requests to view the execution also have to be submitted in writing.

The Oklahoma statute puts no limit to the number of immediate family members who may view the execution. The family member has to be 18 years or older and may be "... the spouse, a child by birth or adoption, a stepchild, a parent, a grandparent, or a sibling of the deceased victim." The family views the execution in an area separate from the other witnesses. If a separate room for direct viewing is not available, a closed-circuit television is provided. On the other hand, in Delaware and Louisiana, only a single family member or representative is allowed to attend the execution.

Eight other states — Florida, Illinois, Montana, North Carolina, Pennsylvania, Texas, Utah, and Virginia — allow victims' families to be present at executions by policy. While Pennsylvania's law specifies that "... six reputable adult citizens ..." may attend the execution, a state policy allows victims' family members to be included in this category. The Texas Board of Criminal Justice has also established a policy letting victims' families attend executions. Only one state, New Jersey, prohibits "... any person who is related by either blood or marriage to the sentenced person or to the victim to be present at the execution...."

Some family members of the murdered victims feel that witnessing the death of their loved ones' murderers has helped put closure to their tragedy. On January 13, 2000, the execution of Oklahoman Gary Allen Walker was watched by the family members of the five victims he had murdered in a 1984 killing spree.

In August 1996, state Senator Brooks Douglass (R-OK) witnessed the execution of Steven Hatch, one of the men who killed his parents, raped his sister, and shot him in the back in 1979. Douglass wrote the state law allowing family members of victims to be present at executions. After Hatch's execution, Senator Douglass stated, "It wasn't revenge; it wasn't retribution. But for the first time since I was 16, I felt some closure. I felt like I had finally put the past behind me. I know it was the right thing." The second person (Glen Ake) convicted for Douglass's parents' murder is serving a life sentence. The Supreme Court, in *Ake v. Oklahoma* (470 U.S. 68, 1985), overturned the man's conviction. (See Chapter IV.)

Media Witnesses

For the first time, in February 1996, California used lethal injection in place of the gas chamber to execute a death row inmate. In 1994, the use of the gas chamber had been ruled cruel and unusual punishment (see Chapter IV). Subsequent to the change in execution method, the Society of Professional Journalists and the California First Amendment Coalition filed suit, claiming that the state had unlawfully limited media access to the execution.

The lawsuit claimed that California's new public witness procedure violated the First Amendment. It prevented the witnesses from observing "the entry, treatment, and restraint of inmates, and the insertion of the lethal injection apparatus." Media witnesses reported that since they were not allowed to see the entire execution, they could not inform the public of the whole process.

In February 1997, the U.S. District Court for the Northern District of California, in *California First Amendment Society v. Calderon*, No. C-96-1291-VRW, ruled that "the First Amendment requires prison officials to allow the public and the media to witness lethal injection from the time just before the prisoner is strapped down to a gurney until after death." The Court found that a long history of access to executions has helped inform the public "on whether the state's 'awesome' power to commit executions was properly exercised."

CHAPTER VI

HISTORICAL STATISTICS*

HOW MANY EXECUTIONS?

From 1930, when the Bureau of Justice Statistics (BJS) national reporting began, through 1998, 4,359 executions were conducted under civil authority in the United States (Figure 6.1 and Table 6.1). Military authorities carried out an additional 160 executions from 1930 to 1998 (not shown). The Death Penalty Information Center reported 98 executions for 1999, the most in one year since the death penalty was reinstated in 1976, making the total 4,457 as of December 31, 1999. (See Figure 6.2.)

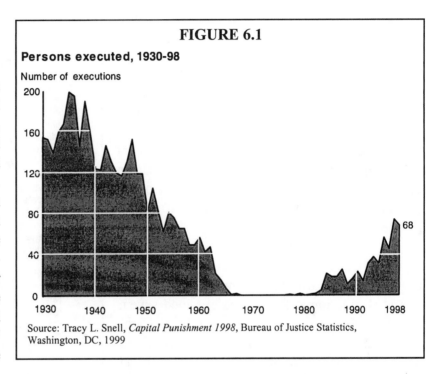

FIGURE 6.1

Persons executed, 1930-98

Number of executions

Source: Tracy L. Snell, *Capital Punishment 1998*, Bureau of Justice Statistics, Washington, DC, 1999

The number of executions generally declined between the 1930s and the 1960s (Figure 6.1). In 1967, a 10-year moratorium (temporary suspension) of the death penalty began as states waited for the Supreme Court to determine a constitutionally acceptable procedure for carrying out the death penalty. (See Chapter II.) After the moratorium

---

* The statistics and charts used in this chapter were prepared by the Bureau of Justice Statistics (BJS) of the U.S. Department of Justice. Additional information was supplied by the NAACP Legal Defense and Educational Fund, Inc. (LDF), of New York, a nationally recognized private organization that collects information on capital punishment. The LDF is no longer a part of the National Association for the Advancement of Colored People (NAACP), although it was founded by that organization and shares its commitment to equal rights and opposition to capital punishment. The LDF has had a separate board of directors, program, staff, office, and budget for over 30 years. The LDF publishes a quarterly, *Death Row, USA*, which reports the total number of death row inmates, the number executed since January 1, 1976, and other information on capital punishment in America. The Death Penalty Information Center (DPIC; Washington, DC) also provided information on capital punishment. A nonprofit organization, the DPIC, which strongly opposes the death penalty, serves as a resource to those who are working on the issue.

ended, the first execution occurred in Utah in 1977. Since 1977, 598 executions had taken place as of December 31, 1999 (Figure 6.2).

WHERE ARE THE EXECUTIONS?

Over the past 50 years, approximately 3 out of every 5 executions took place in the South. Of the 500 executions (BJS data up to 1998) since 1977, all but 59 were in the South. From 1930 to 1998, the largest single number (461), more than 10 percent of the total, occurred in Texas. Forty-five percent of all executions were carried out in just six states — Texas, Georgia, New York, California, North Carolina, and Florida. (See Table 6.1.)

Between 1977 and 1998, 29 states executed prisoners, led by Texas with 164; Virginia with 59; Florida, 43; Missouri, 32; Louisiana, 24; Georgia, 23; and South Carolina, 20. These seven states accounted for three-quarters (73 percent) of all executions during this twenty-one-year period (Table 6.1).

In 1999, Texas had the largest number of executions (35), followed by Virginia (14). Missouri executed nine inmates, Arizona executed seven, and Oklahoma executed six. Arkansas, North Carolina, and South Carolina each put four prisoners to death. Alabama, California, and Delaware each had two executions, while Florida, Illinois, Indiana, Kentucky, Louisiana, Nevada, Ohio, Pennsylvania, and Utah each had one. (See Table 6.2.)

GENDER

Between 1976, when the Supreme Court allowed the death penalty to resume, and September 1, 1999, 563 men and three women were executed (Table 6.3). Between 1930 and 1990 (latest BJS information available), 33 women were put to death (Table 6.4).

In 1984, Margie Velma Barfield was executed in North Carolina for poisoning her boyfriend. Karla Faye Tucker of Texas was convicted of beating two people to death with a pickax. In February 1998, Tucker was the first woman to be executed in Texas since the Civil War. (In 1863, Chipita Rodriguez, the last woman to be executed in Texas, was put to death by hanging.) Judy Buenoano was convicted of poisoning her husband with arsenic. She was also convicted of drowning her paraplegic son and trying to kill her boyfriend. In March 1998, Buenoano was the first woman to be ex-

TABLE 6.1

Number of persons executed, by jurisdiction, 1930-98

State	Number executed	
	Since 1930	Since 1977
U.S. total	4,359	500
Texas	461	164
Georgia	389	23
New York	329	
California	297	5
North Carolina	274	11
Florida	213	43
South Carolina	182	20
Ohio	172	
Mississippi	158	4
Louisiana	157	24
Pennsylvania	154	2
Alabama	152	17
Virginia	151	59
Arkansas	135	17
Kentucky	104	1
Illinois	101	11
Missouri	94	32
Tennessee	93	
New Jersey	74	
Oklahoma	73	13
Maryland	71	3
Arizona	50	12
Washington	50	3
Colorado	48	1
Indiana	47	6
District of Columbia	40	
West Virginia	40	
Nevada	36	7
Federal system	33	
Massachusetts	27	
Oregon	21	2
Connecticut	21	
Delaware	20	8
Utah	18	5
Iowa	18	
Kansas	15	
Montana	8	2
New Mexico	8	
Wyoming	8	1
Nebraska	7	3
Idaho	4	1
Vermont	4	
New Hampshire	1	
South Dakota	1	

Source: Tracy L. Snell, *Capital Punishment 1998*, Bureau of Justice Statistics, Washington, DC, 1999

ecuted in Florida since 1848, when a freed slave named Celia was hanged for killing her master. In February 2000, Betty Lou Beets was executed in Texas for killing her fifth husband.

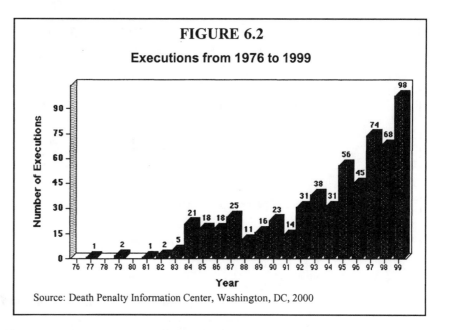

FIGURE 6.2

Executions from 1976 to 1999

Source: Death Penalty Information Center, Washington, DC, 2000

RACE AND ETHNICITY

More than half of those executed between 1930 and 1996 were Black (52 percent), 46.7 percent were White, and 1 percent were categorized as "other" race (Table 6.5). Of the 566 prisoners executed from 1977 to September 1, 1999 (LDF data), 56 percent were White (317), 35 percent were Black (198), 6.5 percent were Hispanic (who may be of any race) (37), 1.6 percent were Native American (9), and nearly one percent were Asian (5). (See Table 6.3.)

The LDF maintains statistics not only on the race of the executed prisoners, but also of their victims (Table 6.3). These types of statistics were used in court cases to decide the constitutionality of the death penalty. The courts had to consider whether Whites who murdered Blacks got lighter sentences than Blacks who murdered Whites and whether those sentences violated the equal protection rights of the Constitution. (See Chapter IV for the outcome of *Turner v. Murray* and *McCleskey v. Kemp* and Chapter VII for race as a consideration in the imposition of the death penalty.)

From 1977 through September 1, 1999, 52.7 percent of those executed were Whites who had murdered other Whites, while 1.9 percent were

TABLE 6.2

NUMBER OF EXECUTIONS BY STATE SINCE 1976

(As of December 31, 1999)
(Total Since 1976: 598; Total for 1999: 98)

STATE	Total	1999	STATE	Total	1999
Texas	199	35	California	7	2
Virginia	73	14	Indiana	7	1
Florida	44	1	Utah	6	1
Missouri	41	9	Mississippi	4	
Louisiana	25	1	Nebraska	3	
S. Carolina	24	4	Washington	3	
Georgia	23		Maryland	3	
Arkansas	21	4	Pennsylvania	3	1
Alabama	19	2	Oregon	2	
Arizona	19	7	Montana	2	
Oklahoma	19	6	Kentucky	2	1
N. Carolina	15	4	Idaho	1	
Illinois	12	1	Wyoming	1	
Delaware	10	2	Colorado	1	
Nevada	8	1	Ohio	1	1

Source: Death Penalty Information Center, Washington, DC, 2000

TABLE 6.3

Execution Update (1977 to September 1, 1999)
Gender

Gender of defendants executed
total number 566

Female .... 3 (.53%)
Male 563 (99.47%)

Gender of victims
total number 756

Female 344 (45.50%)
Male 412 (54.50%)

Race

Race of defendants executed

White 317 (56.01%)
Black 198 (34.98%)
Latino/a 37 (6.54%)
Native American 9 (1.59%)
Asian .... 5 (.88%)

Race of victims

White 619 (81.88%)
Black 93 (12.30%)
Latino/a 27 (3.57%)
Asian 17 (2.25%)

Defendant-victim racial combinations

	White Victim	Black Victim	Latino/a Victim	Asian Victim
White Defendant	298 (52.65%)	11 (1.94%)	3 (.53%)	3 (.53%)
Black Defendant	131 (23.14%)	53 (9.36%)	4 (.71%)	4 (.71%)
Latino/a Defendant	19 (3.36%)	2 (.35%)	14 (2.47%)	1 (.18%)
Asian Defendant	1 (.18%)	0 (0%)	0 (0%)	4 (.71%)
Native American	8 (1.41%)	0 (0%)	0 (0%)	0 (0%)

Note: In addition, there were 10 defendants executed for the murders of multiple victims of different races.
Of those, 5 defendants were black, 3 white, 1 Latin and 1 Native American. (1.77%)

Source: *Death Row, U.S.A.*, Fall 1999, NAACP Legal Defense and Educational Fund, Inc., New York, NY, 1999

TABLE 6.4

Female prisoners executed under civil authority

By offense, race, and jurisdiction, United States, 1930-90

(- represents zero)

Year	Total	Offense		Race		Jurisdiction in which executed
		Murder	Other[a]	White	Black	
1930-90	33	31	2	21	12	X
1984	1	1	-	1	-	North Carolina
1962	1	1	-	1	-	California
1957	1	1	-	1	-	Alabama
1955	1	1	-	1	-	California
1954	2	2	-	1	1	Ohio
1953	3	1	2	3	-	Alabama, Federal (Missouri and New York)
1951	1	1	-	1	-	New York
1947	2	2	-	1	1	California, South Carolina
1946	1	1	-	-	1	Pennsylvania
1945	1	1	-	-	1	Georgia
1944	3	3	-	-	3	Mississippi, New York, North Carolina
1943	3	3	-	1	2	Mississippi, North Carolina, South Carolina
1942	1	1	-	1	-	Louisiana
1941	1	1	-	1	-	California
1938	2	2	-	2	-	Illinois, Ohio
1937	1	1	-	-	1	Mississippi
1936	1	1	-	1	-	New York
1935	3	3	-	2	1	Delaware, Louisiana, New York
1934	1	1	-	1	-	New York
1931	1	1	-	1	-	Pennsylvania
1930	2	2	-	1	1	Arizona, Alabama

No females were executed in the years that are not listed.

[a]Includes one kidnaping and one espionage case (both Federal).

Source: U.S. Department of Justice, Bureau of Justice Statistics. *Capital Punishment 1984*, NCJ-99562, Table 4; *1986*, Bulletin NCJ-106483, p. 9, Appendix table 2, *1988*, Bulletin NCJ-118313, p. 2; *1989*, Bulletin NCJ-124545, p. 2 (Washington, DC: U.S. Department of Justice). Table adapted by SOURCEBOOK staff.

TABLE 6.5

Prisoners executed under civil authority

By race and offense, United States, 1930-96

(- represents zero)

	Total				White				Black				Other			
	Total	Murder	Rape	Other offenses[a]	Total	Murder	Rape	Other offenses	Total	Murder	Rape	Other offenses	Total	Murder	Rape	Other offenses
1930-96	4,217	3,692	455	70	1,971	1,884	48	39	2,201	1,765	405	31	45	43	2	-
1996	45	45	-	-	31	31	-	-	14	14	-	-	-	-	-	-
1995	56	56	-	-	33	33	-	-	22	22	-	-	1	1	-	-
1994	31	31	-	-	20	20	-	-	11	11	-	-	-	-	-	-
1993	38.0	38	-	-	23	23	-	-	14	14	-	-	1	1	-	-
1992	31.0	31	-	-	19	19	-	-	11	11	-	-	1	1	-	-
1991	14	14	-	-	7	7	-	-	7	7	-	-	-	-	-	-
1990	23	23	-	-	16	16	-	-	7	7	-	-	-	-	-	-
1989	16	16	-	-	8	8	-	-	8	8	-	-	-	-	-	-
1988	11	11	-	-	6	6	-	-	5	5	-	-	-	-	-	-
1987	25	25	-	-	13	13	-	-	12	12	-	-	-	-	-	-
1986	18	18	-	-	11	11	-	-	7	7	-	-	-	-	-	-
1985	18	18	-	-	11	11	-	-	7	7	-	-	-	-	-	-
1984	21	21	-	-	13	13	-	-	8	8	-	-	-	-	-	-
1983	5	5	-	-	4	4	-	-	1	1	-	-	-	-	-	-
1982	2	2	-	-	1	1	-	-	1	1	-	-	-	-	-	-
1981	1	1	-	-	1	1	-	-	-	-	-	-	-	-	-	-
1980	-	-	-	-	-	-	-	-	-	-	-	-	-	-	-	-
1979	2	2	-	-	2	2	-	-	-	-	-	-	-	-	-	-
1978	-	-	-	-	-	-	-	-	-	-	-	-	-	-	-	-
1977[b]	1	1	-	-	1	1	-	-	-	-	-	-	-	-	-	-
1967	2	2	-	-	1	1	-	-	1	1	-	-	-	-	-	-
1966	1	1	-	-	1	1	-	-	-	-	-	-	-	-	-	-
1965	7	7	-	-	6	6	-	-	1	1	-	-	-	-	-	-
1964	15	9	6	-	8	5	3	-	7	4	3	-	-	-	-	-
1963	21	18	2	1	13	12	-	1	8	6	2	-	-	-	-	-
1962	47	41	4	2	28	26	2	-	19	15	2	2	-	-	-	-
1961	42	33	8	1	20	18	1	1	22	15	7	-	-	-	-	-
1960	56	44	8	4	21	18	-	3	35	26	8	1	-	-	-	-
1959	49	41	8	-	16	15	1	-	33	26	7	-	-	-	-	-
1958	49	41	7	1	20	20	-	-	28	20	7	1	1	1	-	-
1957	65	54	10	1	34	32	2	-	31	22	8	1	-	-	-	-
1956	65	52	12	1	21	20	-	1	43	31	12	-	1	1	-	-
1955	76	65	7	4	44	41	1	2	32	24	6	2	-	-	-	-
1954	81	71	9	1	38	37	1	-	42	33	8	1	1	1	-	-
1953	62	51	7	4	30	25	1	4	31	25	6	-	1	1	-	-
1952	83	71	12	-	36	35	1	-	47	36	11	-	-	-	-	-
1951	105	87	17	1	57	55	2	-	47	31	15	1	1	1	-	-
1950	82	68	13	1	40	36	4	-	42	32	9	1	-	-	-	-
1949	119	107	10	2	50	49	-	1	67	56	10	1	2	2	-	-
1948	119	95	22	2	35	32	1	2	82	61	21	-	2	2	-	-
1947	153	129	23	1	42	40	2	-	111	89	21	1	-	-	-	-
1946	131	107	22	2	46	45	-	1	84	61	22	1	1	1	-	-
1945	117	90	26	1	41	37	4	-	75	52	22	1	1	1	-	-
1944	120	96	24	-	47	45	2	-	70	48	22	-	3	3	-	-
1943	131	118	13	-	54	54	-	-	74	63	11	-	3	1	2	-
1942	147	115	25	7	67	57	4	6	80	58	21	1	-	-	-	-
1941	123	102	20	1	59	55	4	-	63	46	16	1	1	1	-	-
1940	124	105	15	4	49	44	2	3	75	61	13	1	-	-	-	-
1939	160	145	12	3	80	79	-	1	77	63	12	2	3	3	-	-
1938	190	154	25	11	96	89	1	6	92	63	24	5	2	2	-	-
1937	147	133	13	1	69	67	2	-	74	62	11	1	4	4	-	-
1936	195	181	10	4	92	86	2	4	101	93	8	-	2	2	-	-
1935	199	184	13	2	119	115	2	2	77	66	11	-	3	3	-	-
1934	168	154	14	-	65	64	1	-	102	89	13	-	1	1	-	-
1933	160	151	7	2	77	75	1	1	81	74	6	1	2	2	-	-
1932	140	128	10	2	62	62	-	-	75	63	10	2	3	3	-	-
1931	153	137	15	1	77	76	1	-	72	57	14	1	4	4	-	-
1930	155	147	6	2	90	90	-	-	65	57	6	2	-	-	-	-

Note: See Note, table 6.92. For information on methodology, definitions of terms, and explanatory notes, see Appendix 4.

Source: U.S. Department of Justice, Bureau of Justice Statistics, *Correctional Populations in the United States, 1996*, NCJ-170013 (Washington, DC: U.S. Department of Justice, 1999), p. 173. Table adapted by SOURCEBOOK staff.

[a]Includes 25 executed for armed robbery, 20 for kidnaping, 11 for burglary, 6 for sabotage, 6 for aggravated assault, and 2 for espionage.
[b]There were no executions from 1968 through 1976;

Source: Kathleen Maguire and Ann L. Pastore, eds., *Sourcebook of Criminal Justice Statistics 1998*, Bureau of Justice Statistics, Washington, DC, 1999

Whites who had murdered Black persons. Twenty-three percent of those executed were Blacks who had murdered Whites, and 9.4 percent were Blacks who had murdered other Blacks. (See Table 6.3.)

CRIMES COMMITTED

The vast majority of executions from 1930 through 1996 were for murder (88 percent), followed by rape (11 percent). The remaining 1 percent of executions included 25 cases for armed robbery, 20 for kidnapping, 11 for burglary, 6 for sabotage, 6 for aggravated assault, and 2 for espionage. Since 1965, all those executed have been convicted on murder charges. (See Table 6.5.)

The last execution for rape occurred in 1964. In 1977, in *Coker v. Georgia* (433 U.S. 584), the Supreme Court ruled that rape did not warrant the death penalty (see Chapter III). In December 1996, however, the Louisiana Supreme Court ruled that death is a just and constitutional punishment for the rape of a child under 12 years of age (*Lousiana v. Wilson,* 1996 WL 718217). Currently, Louisiana is the only state with such a law. (See Table 5.1 in Chapter V.) This issue will eventually be decided by the U.S. Supreme Court.

METHOD OF EXECUTION

Among the 500 prisoners executed between 1977 and 1998, most (344) received lethal injections, followed by electrocution (141). Ten executions were carried out by lethal gas, three by hang-

ing, and two by firing squad. Texas, the state with the largest number of prisoners executed, used lethal injection in all of its 164 cases. Virginia executed 34 death row inmates, using lethal injecton, and 25 inmates, using electrocution. Florida used electrocution to execute its 43 prisoners. (See Table 6.6.)

TABLE 6.6

Executions, by State and method, 1977-98

State	Number executed	Lethal injection	Electro-cution	Lethal gas	Firing squad	Hanging
Total	500	344	141	10	2	3
Alabama	17	0	17	0	0	0
Arizona	12	11	0	1	0	0
Arkansas	17	16	1	0	0	0
California	5	3	0	2	0	0
Colorado	1	1	0	0	0	0
Delaware	8	7	0	0	0	1
Florida	43	0	43	0	0	0
Georgia	23	0	23	0	0	0
Idaho	1	1	0	0	0	0
Illinois	11	11	0	0	0	0
Indiana	6	3	3	0	0	0
Kentucky	1	0	1	0	0	0
Louisiana	24	4	20	0	0	0
Maryland	3	3	0	0	0	0
Mississippi	4	0	0	4	0	0
Missouri	32	32	0	0	0	0
Montana	2	2	0	0	0	0
Nebraska	3	0	3	0	0	0
Nevada	7	6	0	1	0	0
North Carolina	11	9	0	2	0	0
Oklahoma	13	13	0	0	0	0
Oregon	2	2	0	0	0	0
Pennsylvania	2	2	0	0	0	0
South Carolina	20	15	5	0	0	0
Texas	164	164	0	0	0	0
Utah	5	3	0	0	2	0
Virginia	59	34	25	0	0	0
Washington	3	1	0	0	0	2
Wyoming	1	1	0	0	0	0

Note: These tables show the distributions of execution methods used since 1977. Lethal injection was used in 69% of the executions carried out. Eleven States — Arizona, Arkansas, California, Delaware, Indiana, Louisiana, Nevada, North Carolina, South Carolina, Utah, and Virginia — have employed 2 methods.

Source: Tracy L. Snell, *Capital Punishment 1998*, Bureau of Justice Statistics, Washington, DC, 1999

CHAPTER VII

UNDER SENTENCE OF DEATH*

AN EVER-INCREASING NUMBER

At yearend 1998, the Bureau of Justice Statistics reported a total of 3,452 prisoners held under sentence of death in federal and state prisons — a 4 percent increase over the previous year. The number of prisoners on death row has been increasing for more than 20 years (Figure 7.1).

The continually growing number of prisoners on death row reflects a rise in the number of death sentences being imposed. Moreover, just a small number of prisoners is removed from death row for reasons other than execution — resentencing, retrial, commutation, or death while awaiting execution (natural death, murder, or suicide).

While appeals often used to be lengthy, the 1996 Anti-Terrorism and Effective Death Penalty Act (PL 104-132) has reduced the number of appeals inmates can make to federal courts (see Chapter I). Consequently, the number of executions will likely be on the rise. However, the current increase

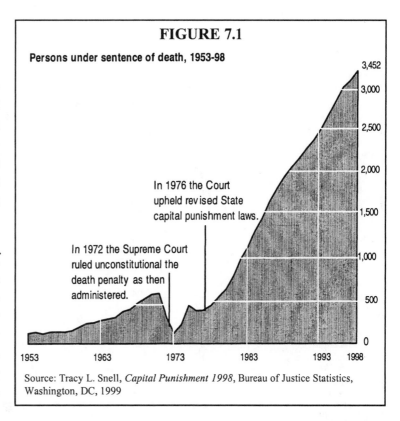

FIGURE 7.1

Persons under sentence of death, 1953-98

In 1976 the Court upheld revised State capital punishment laws.

In 1972 the Supreme Court ruled unconstitutional the death penalty as then administered.

Source: Tracy L. Snell, *Capital Punishment 1998*, Bureau of Justice Statistics, Washington, DC, 1999

in the number of executions is more a product of inmates' appeals being exhausted than the new law.

From 1973 to 1998, 6,431 persons received the death sentence. Of these, 500 were executed, 180 died while awaiting execution, 2,124 had their sentences or convictions overturned, and 146 had their

---

* Statistical information on capital punishment comes mainly from two different sources that update their material at varying times. The Bureau of Justice Statistics *Capital Punishment 1998* (Washington, DC, December 1999) gives information through December 1998. The NAACP Legal Defense and Educational Fund, Inc. (LDF), a non-profit organization that collects information on capital punishment, publishes a semi-annual release, *Death Row, U.S.A.*, the latest of which offers information through September 1, 1999.

sentences commuted. As of December 31, 1998, over half (54 percent) were still on death row awaiting execution. (See Table 7.1.)

Between January 1 and December 31, 1998, 30 states received 285 prisoners under sentence of death. The Federal Bureau of Prisons received five

TABLE 7.1

Number sentenced to death and number of removals, by jurisdiction and reason for removal, 1973-98

State	Total sentenced to death, 1973-98	Number of removals, 1973-98					Under sentence of death, 12/31/98
		Executed	Died	Sentence or conviction overturned	Sentence commuted	Other removals	
U.S. total	6,431	500	180	2,124	146	29	3,452
Federal	21	0	0	2	0	0	19
Alabama	302	17	11	95	1	0	178
Arizona	217	12	8	71	5	1	120
Arkansas	89	17	1	30	1	0	40
California	679	5	30	117	15	0	512
Colorado	16	1	1	10	1	0	3
Connecticut	6	0	0	1	0	0	5
Delaware	38	8	0	13	0	0	17
Florida	802	43	22	345	18	2	372
Georgia	281	23	8	134	6	1	109
Idaho	36	1	1	13	2	0	19
Illinois	264	11	9	79	1	7	157
Indiana	90	6	1	34	2	2	45
Kansas	1	0	0	0	0	0	1
Kentucky	66	1	2	26	1	0	36
Louisiana	184	24	3	75	6	1	75
Maryland	47	3	1	24	2	0	17
Massachusetts	4	0	0	2	2	0	0
Mississippi	159	4	1	86	0	3	65
Missouri	151	32	7	21	1	0	90
Montana	15	2	0	6	1	0	6
Nebraska	24	3	2	6	2	0	11
Nevada	123	7	5	24	3	0	84
New Jersey	47	0	2	23	0	8	14
New Mexico	26	0	1	16	5	0	4
New York	4	0	0	3	0	0	1
North Carolina	448	11	8	238	4	0	187
Ohio	341	0	8	133	9	0	191
Oklahoma	290	13	7	125	1	0	144
Oregon	44	2	1	18	0	0	23
Pennsylvania	303	2	8	69	0	0	224
Rhode Island	2	0	0	2	0	0	0
South Carolina	159	20	4	64	3	0	68
South Dakota	2	0	0	0	0	0	2
Tennessee	184	0	5	80	0	2	97
Texas	780	164	18	101	45	1	451
Utah	25	5	0	9	1	0	10
Virginia	116	59	3	6	8	1	39
Washington	34	3	1	16	0	0	14
Wyoming	11	1	1	7	0	0	2
Percent	100%	7.8%	2.8%	33.0%	2.3%	0.5%	53.7%

Note: For those persons sentenced to death more than once, the numbers are based on the most recent death sentence.

Source: Tracy L. Snell, *Capital Punishment 1998*, Bureau of Justice Statistics, Washington, DC, 1999

inmates. Of these prisoners, 256 had been convicted of murder. Eighty prisoners from 22 states had their death sentences overturned or removed. Florida reported the most numbers (16) of vacated (annulled) capital sentences.

In fall 1999, the NAACP Legal Defense and Educational Fund, Inc. (LDF), reported 3,625 prisoners under sentence of death. The LDF statistics include persons who have been sentenced to death and are awaiting transfer to prison, while the Bureau of Justice Statistics counts only those on death row awaiting execution.

GEOGRAPHIC DISTRIBUTION

As of December 31, 1998, more than half (55.2 percent) of the state prisoners awaiting execution were in the South. An additional 23.2 percent were in Western states, and 14.4 percent were in Midwestern states. The Northeastern states of Connecticut, New Hampshire, New Jersey, New York, and Pennsylvania accounted for the remaining 7.1 percent. About 39 percent of the condemned were awaiting execution in three states — California (512), Texas (451), and Florida (372). Of the 38 jurisdictions with statutes authorizing the death penalty, only New Hampshire had no one under a capital sentence, while Colorado, Kansas, New Mexico, New York, South Dakota, and Wyoming had four or fewer. (See Table 7.2.)

Between January 1 and December 31, 1998, of the 30 state and federal prison systems that received prisoners (290 total, see above) under sentence of death, Texas (39), California (31), Florida (25), and Alabama (25) accounted for 41.4 percent of the inmates sentenced to death.

GENDER AND RACE

As of 1998, about 99 percent (3,404) of all prisoners under sentence of death were males (Table 7.3). Forty-eight females were awaiting execution, up from 35 in 1990. (In 1998, eight women were received in the prison systems; however, two were removed from death row and two were executed. See Chapter VI.) Of these women, 29 were White

Region and State	Prisoners under sentence of death, 12/31/98		
	Total	White	Black
U.S. total	3,452	1,906	1,486
Federal	19	6	13
State	3,433	1,900	1,473
Northeast	244	85	148
Connecticut	5	2	3
New Hampshire	0	0	0
New Jersey	14	8	6
New York	1	0	1
Pennsylvania	224	75	138
Midwest	497	239	256
Illinois	157	58	99
Indiana	45	30	15
Kansas	1	1	0
Missouri	90	46	44
Nebraska	11	9	1
Ohio	191	93	97
South Dakota	2	2	0
South	1,895	1,045	827
Alabama	178	95	82
Arkansas	40	20	20
Delaware	17	7	10
Florida	372	241	131
Georgia	109	56	52
Kentucky	36	28	8
Louisiana	75	23	52
Maryland	17	5	12
Mississippi	65	28	37
North Carolina	187	79	102
Oklahoma	144	89	47
South Carolina	68	33	35
Tennessee	97	62	33
Texas	451	257	189
Virginia	39	22	17
West	797	531	242
Arizona	120	103	11
California	512	310	188
Colorado	3	1	2
Idaho	19	19	0
Montana	6	5	0
Nevada	84	48	35
New Mexico	4	4	0
Oregon	23	22	0
Utah	10	7	2
Washington	14	10	4
Wyoming	2	2	0

Source: Tracy L. Snell, *Capital Punishment 1998*, Bureau of Justice Statistics, Washington, DC, 1999

and 17 were Black. Half (54 percent) of these women were in California (10), Texas (8), Florida (4), and Pennsylvania (4). (See Tables 7.4 and 7.5.) In fall 1999, the LDF reported 3,575 males and 50 females in death row.

TABLE 7.3

Demographic characteristics of prisoners under sentence of death, 1998

Characteristic	Yearend	Admissions	Removals
	Prisoners under sentence of death, 1998		
Total number under sentence of death	3,452	285	161
Gender			
Male	98.6%	97.2%	97.5%
Female	1.4	2.8	2.5
Race			
White	55.2%	50.9%	64.0%
Black	43.0	46.3	33.5
Other*	1.7	2.8	2.5
Hispanic origin			
Hispanic	10.0%	15.4%	10.2%
Non-Hispanic	90.0	84.6	89.8
Education			
8th grade or less	14.3%	15.1%	17.1%
9th-11th grade	37.6	39.3	37.1
High school graduate/GED	38.0	36.8	37.1
Any college	10.1	8.8	8.6
Median	11th	11th	11th
Marital status			
Married	24.0%	17.1%	23.6%
Divorced/separated	20.8	16.0	22.3
Widowed	2.7	4.7	4.1
Never married	52.5	62.3	50.0

Note: Calculations are based on those cases for which data were reported. Missing data by category were as follows:

	Yearend	Admissions	Removals
Hispanic origin	299	38	14
Education	501	46	21
Marital status	327	28	13

*At yearend 1997, "other" consisted of 28 American Indians, 17 Asians, and 11 self-identified Hispanics. During 1998, 3 American Indians, 2 Asians, and 3 self-identified Hispanics were admitted; 2 American Indians, 1 Asian, and 1 self-identified Hispanic were removed.

Source: Tracy L. Snell, *Capital Punishment 1998*, Bureau of Justice Statistics, Washington, DC, 1999

TABLE 7.4

Women under sentence of death, 12/31/98

State	Total	White	Black
Total	48	29	17
California	10	6	2
Texas	8	5	3
Florida	4	2	2
Pennsylvania	4	1	3
North Carolina	3	3	0
Alabama	3	2	1
Oklahoma	3	2	1
Illinois	3	0	3
Tennessee	2	2	0
Missouri	1	1	0
Arkansas	1	1	0
Georgia	1	1	0
Mississippi	1	1	0
Arizona	1	1	0
Idaho	1	1	0
Indiana	1	0	1
Nevada	1	0	1

Source: Tracy L. Snell, *Capital Punishment 1998*, Bureau of Justice Statistics, Washington, DC, 1999

311 Hispanics (8.6 percent), 46 Native Americans (1.3 percent), and 31 Asians (less than 1 percent) were under sentence of death. Seven inmates were of unknown race.

CHARACTERISTICS OF PRISONERS

In 1998, the median age (half were younger and half were older) of those under sentence of death was 37 years. Seven in 10 (69 percent) were ages 25 to 44, and 4 of 10 (37.5 percent) were between 30 and 39 years old. Few were under 20 years old (8.1 percent) or over 55 years (5 percent). The youngest inmate was 18 years old and was sentenced to death in December 1998. The oldest was 83, having been sentenced in June 1983 at the age of 68. Half of all inmates under sentence of death were ages 20 to 29 when they were arrested for their capital offense. (See Table 7.6.)

Half (55.2 percent) of all death row inmates were White, and 43 percent were Black. Hispanic prisoners (314), whose ethnicity was known and who may be of any race, accounted for 10 percent of those under a death sentence. (See Tables 7.3 and 7.5.) Eight in 10 (80.6 percent) of the 314 Hispanics sentenced to death were imprisoned in four states — California (97), Texas (93), Florida (43), and Arizona (20). (See Table 7.5.)

According to the LDF, as of fall 1999, 1,686 Whites (46.5 percent), 1,544 Blacks (42.6 percent),

Among those for whom information about education was available, more than half (51.9 percent)

TABLE 7.5

Hispanics and women under sentence of death, by State, 1997 and 1998

Region and State	Under sentence of death, 12/31/97 Hispanics	Women	Received under sentence of death Hispanics	Women	Death sentence removed* Hispanics	Women	Under sentence of death, 12/31/98 Hispanics	Women
U.S. total	291	44	38	8	15	4	314	48
Alabama	0	3	0	0	0	0	0	3
Arizona	20	1	3	0	3	0	20	1
Arkansas	1	0	0	1	0	0	1	1
California	80	8	17	2	0	0	97	10
Colorado	1	0	0	0	0	0	1	0
Florida	41	6	4	0	2	2	43	4
Georgia	1	0	0	1	0	0	1	1
Idaho	0	1	0	0	0	0	0	1
Illinois	9	2	0	1	1	0	8	3
Indiana	2	0	0	1	0	0	2	1
Louisiana	1	0	0	0	0	0	1	0
Mississippi	1	1	0	0	0	0	1	1
Missouri	0	1	0	0	0	0	0	1
Nevada	8	1	0	0	0	0	8	1
New Jersey	0	1	0	0	0	1	0	0
New Mexico	1	0	0	0	0	0	1	0
North Carolina	4	3	0	0	1	0	3	3
Ohio	5	0	0	0	0	0	5	0
Oklahoma	7	3	0	0	0	0	7	3
Oregon	2	0	0	0	0	0	2	0
Pennsylvania	15	4	2	0	0	0	17	4
Tennessee	1	2	0	0	0	0	1	2
Texas	88	7	12	2	7	1	93	8
Utah	2	0	0	0	0	0	2	0
Virginia	1	0	0	0	1	0	1	0

*Eight Hispanic men were executed in 1998 (5 in Texas, 2 in Arizona, and 1 in Virginia).
Two women were executed during 1998 (1 each in Florida and Texas).

TABLE 7.6

**Age at time of arrest for capital offense and
age of prisoners under sentence of death at yearend 1998**

Age	Prisoners under sentence of death			
	At time of arrest Number*	Percent	On December 31, 1998 Number	Percent
Total number under sentence of death on 12/31/98	3,158	100 %	3,452	100 %
17 or younger	72	2.3	0	
18-19	340	10.8	15	0.4
20-24	856	27.1	267	7.7
25-29	727	23.0	519	15.0
30-34	510	16.1	582	16.9
35-39	336	10.6	711	20.6
40-44	160	5.1	578	16.7
45-49	94	3.0	352	10.2
50-54	36	1.1	258	7.5
55-59	17	0.5	99	2.9
60 or older	10	0.3	71	2.1
Mean age	28 yrs		38 yrs	
Median age	26 yrs		37 yrs	

Note: The youngest person under sentence of death was a black male in Alabama,
born in July 1980 and sentenced to death in December 1998. The oldest person
under sentence of death was a white male in Arizona, born in September 1915 and
sentenced to death in June 1983.
*Excludes 294 inmates for whom the date of arrest for capital offense was not available.

Source of both tables: Tracy L. Snell, *Capital Punishment 1998*, Bureau of Justice Statistics, Washington, DC, 1999

TABLE 7.7

Criminal history profile of prisoners under sentence of death, by race and Hispanic origin, 1998

	Prisoners under sentence of death							
	Number				Percent[a]			
	All[b]	White	Black	Hispanic	All[b]	White	Black	Hispanic
U.S. total	3,452	1,621	1,472	314	100%	100%	100%	100%
Prior felony convictions								
Yes	2,060	933	932	171	65.0%	62.6%	68.9%	60.9%
No	1,107	557	421	110	35.0	37.4	31.1	39.1
Not reported	285							
Prior homicide convictions								
Yes	291	132	130	23	8.6%	8.3%	9.1%	7.5%
No	3,085	1,458	1,306	283	91.4	91.7	90.9	92.5
Not reported	76							
Legal status at time of capital offense								
Charges pending	219	118	87	12	7.2%	8.2%	6.8%	4.6%
Probation	301	137	136	24	9.9	9.5	10.6	9.2
Parole	550	222	257	62	18.1	15.3	20.0	23.8
Prison escapee	39	24	11	3	1.3	1.7	0.9	1.2
Incarcerated	88	37	45	4	2.9	2.6	3.5	1.5
Other status	26	15	9	1	0.9	1.0	0.7	0.4
None	1,810	894	741	154	59.7	61.8	57.6	59.2
Not reported	419							

[a]Percentages are based on those offenders for whom data were reported.
Detail may not add to total because of rounding.
[b]Includes persons of other races.

Source: Tracy L. Snell, *Capital Punishment 1998*, Bureau of Justice Statistics, Washington, DC, 1999

in prison, had escaped from prison, or had some other criminal justice status. (See Table 7.7.)

Criminal history patterns varied slightly by race and Hispanic origin. Blacks (68.9 percent) had somewhat more prior felony convictions than Whites (62.6 percent) and Hispanics (60.9 percent). About the same proportion of Blacks (9.1 percent), Whites (8.3 percent), and Hispanics (7.5 percent) had a prior homicide conviction. A somewhat higher proportion of Hispanics (23.8 percent) and Blacks (20 percent) than Whites (15.3 percent) were on parole when arrested for their capital crime. (See Table 7.7.)

Since 1988, information has been collected on the number of death sentences imposed on the offenders entering the prison system. Among the 3,169 individuals admitted under sentence of death

had not graduated from high school, and only one in 10 had any college education. The median level of education was the eleventh grade. Most had never married (52.5 percent), and about one-fourth (23.5 percent) were separated, divorced, or widowed. (See Table 7.3.)

CRIMINAL HISTORY OF DEATH ROW INMATES

On December 31, 1998, among prisoners on death row, two-thirds (65 percent) had prior felony convictions. Almost 1 in 11 (8.6 percent) had been previously convicted of murder or manslaughter. About 2 of 5 (39.4 percent) had an active criminal justice record at the time of the murder for which they were condemned. Almost half of those with an active criminal record were out on parole when they committed their crimes, and one-fourth were on probation. The others had charges pending, were

TABLE 7.8

Number of death sentences received	Inmates
Total	100%
1	85
2	10
3 or more	5
Number admitted under sentence of death, 1988-98	3,169

Source: Tracy L. Snell, *Capital Punishment 1998*, Bureau of Justice Statistics, Washington, DC, 1999

from 1988 to 1998, nearly 1 in every 7 was admitted with two or more death sentences (Table 7.8).

A LONG WAIT

It can be a long wait on death row. Between 1977 and 1998, a total of 6,089 offenders had been under a death sentence for varying periods of time. Of these, 500 (8.2 percent) were actually executed. Another 2,137 (35.1 percent) were removed from under a death sentence by appellate court decisions and reviews or commutations, or had died while awaiting execution. (See Table 7.9.)

For those executed from 1977 to 1998, the average time between the imposition of the most recent death sentence and the execution was about nine years and five months. White prisoners had waited an average of nine years, and Black prisoners, 10 years and three months before their execution. In 1998, the 68 inmates executed were under sentence of death for an average of 10 years and 10 months. (See Table 7.10.)

Of the 3,452 persons under sentence of death on December 31, 1998, 69 (2 percent) were sentenced prior to 1980. Nebraska, Tennessee, Idaho, and Indiana housed the inmates who had served the longest among all condemned inmates. On the other hand, South Dakota had no inmates under sentence of death prior to 1992; New Mexico, prior to 1994; and Wyoming, New York, and Kansas,

prior to 1998. By December 31, 1998, the average time spent under sentence of death by the 3,452 condemned inmates was seven years and four months (Table 7.11), up three months from 1997.

GETTING OFF DEATH ROW

Table 7.12 shows the means by which prisoners can get off death row. The table breaks down the outcome of the sentences for those condemned to death row for the period 1973 through 1998.

TABLE 7.9

Prisoners under sentence of death who were executed or received other dispositions, by race and Hispanic origin, 1977-98

Race/Hispanic origin[b]	Total under sentence of death, 1977-98[c]	Prisoners executed		Prisoners who received other dispositions[a]	
		Number	Percent of total	Number	Percent of total
Total	6,089	500	8.2%	2,137	35.1%
White	3,015	281	9.3%	1,113	36.9%
Black	2,527	178	7.0	877	34.7
Hispanic	464	34	7.3	116	25.0
Other	83	7	8.4	31	37.3

[a]Includes persons removed from under a sentence of death because of statutes struck down on appeal, sentences or convictions vacated, commutations, or death other than by execution.
[b]White, black, and other categories exclude Hispanics.
[c]Includes persons sentenced to death prior to 1977 who were still under sentence of death on 12/31/98 (11), persons sentenced to death prior to 1977 whose death sentence was removed between 1977 and 12/31/98 (369), and persons sentenced to death between 1977 and 12/31/98 (5,709).

TABLE 7.10

Time under sentence of death and execution, by race, 1977-98

Year of execution	Number executed			Average elapsed time from sentence to execution for:		
	All races*	White	Black	All races*	White	Black
Total	500	313	180	113 mos	108 mos.	123 mos.
1977-83	11	9	2	51 mos.	49 mos.	58 mos.
1984	21	13	8	74	76	71
1985	18	11	7	71	65	80
1986	18	11	7	87	78	102
1987	25	13	12	86	78	96
1888	11	6	5	80	72	89
1989	16	8	8	95	78	112
1990	23	16	7	95	97	91
1991	14	7	7	116	124	107
1992	31	19	11	114	104	135
1993	38	23	14	113	112	121
1994	31	20	11	122	117	132
1995	56	33	22	134	128	144
1996	45	31	14	125	112	153
1997	74	45	27	133	126	147
1998	68	48	18	130	128	132

Note: Average time was calculated from the most recent sentencing date.
*Includes American Indians and Asians.

Source of both tables: Tracy L. Snell, *Capital Punishment 1998*, Bureau of Justice Statistics, Washington, DC, 1999

65

TABLE 7.11

Prisoners under sentence of death on December 31, 1998, by State and year of sentencing

State	Year of sentence for prisoners sentenced to and remaining on death row, 12/31/98												Under sentence of death 12/31/98	Average number of years under sentence of death as of 12/31/98
	1974-79	1980-81	1982-83	1984-85	1986-87	1988-89	1990-91	1992-93	1994-95	1996	1997	1998		
Florida	25	11	18	31	32	39	52	46	54	21	18	25	372	8.6
Texas	12	14	13	21	38	50	44	64	86	36	34	39	451	7.1
California	9	17	46	37	45	64	54	73	59	40	37	31	512	8.1
Georgia	7	3	6	5	14	9	11	11	14	6	12	11	109	8.1
Tennessee	4	7	8	12	15	10	12	5	8	5	7	4	97	9.9
Arizona	3	5	10	11	6	14	18	20	13	5	9	6	120	8.5
Nevada	2	4	9	7	4	12	9	2	16	11	6	2	84	8.2
Nebraska	2	2		1	1	1			1	2	1		11	11.3
Illinois	1	12	14	13	13	16	19	21	20	14	7	7	157	8.6
Alabama	1	3	13	9	16	17	11	14	36	17	16	25	178	6.5
North Carolina	1	3	4	4			13	46	50	24	22	20	187	4.6
Arkansas	1		1		2	2	2	8	10	5	5	4	40	5.2
Kentucky	1	1	8	2	4	1	2	4	3	2	3	5	36	8.8
Indiana		2	4	8	6	3	5	5	5	3	1	3	45	9.2
Mississippi		2	4		3	2	10	11	8	9	8	8	65	5.7
Pennsylvania		1	14	16	28	35	20	30	43	14	11	12	224	7.6
Oklahoma		1	6	15	20	15	16	9	19	17	11	15	144	7.1
Maryland		1		3		2	1	1	1	6		2	17	6.8
Ohio			10	30	21	18	20	22	27	17	10	16	191	7.6
Missouri			3	7	11	6	11	11	18	8	9	6	90	6.6
Louisiana			2	6	7	1	2	10	17	8	13	9	75	5.1
Idaho			2	4	1	4	2	2	1	1	1	1	19	9.4
South Carolina			2	3	5	5	8	9	16	8	4	8	68	5.8
Utah			1	2		3	1	1		1	1		10	8.9
Montana			1		1			2		2			6	*
Delaware			1			1		9			4	2	17	5.1
Virginia					2		5	5	13	1	4	9	39	4
New Jersey					1		2	1	4	3	2	1	14	4.4
Colorado					1				1	1			3	*
Washington							2	2	3	1	3	3	14	3.5
Connecticut							2	1	1		1		5	*
Oregon							1	6	7	3	3	3	23	3.7
Federal system							1	4	2	4	3	5	19	2.6
South Dakota								1			1		2	*
New Mexico									2	2			4	*
Wyoming											1		1	*
New York											1		1	*
Kansas											1		1	*
Total	69	89	200	247	297	330	356	456	558	297	268	285	3,452	7.4

Note: For those persons sentenced to death more than once, the numbers are based on the most recent death sentence.
*Averages not calculated for fewer than 10 inmates.

Source: Tracy L. Snell, *Capital Punishment 1998*, Bureau of Justice Statistics, Washington, DC, 1999

During this period, 500 (7.8 percent) were executed. One-third (2,124) of those who left death row got off because of an appeals or higher-court action. Some (146) had their sentences commuted, while another 180 died while awaiting execution.

Using a single year as an example, of the 252 persons sentenced to death in 1990, 12 were executed, 6 died while in confinement, 68 had their convictions or sentences overturned (conviction and sentencing are two separate trials under the two-part system required in death penalty cases.

See Chapter II, *Gregg v. Georgia*). Of the 252 prisoners sentenced in 1990, 165 were still on death row on December 31, 1998.

AUTOMATIC REVIEW

At yearend 1998, among the 38 states with capital punishment statutes, 36 states provided for automatic review of all death sentences regardless of the defendant's wishes. Of the remaining two states, Arkansas had no specific provisions for automatic review, while South Carolina allowed

TABLE 7.12

Prisoners sentenced to death and the outcome sentence, by year of sentencing, 1973-98

Year of sentence	Number sentenced to death	Number of prisoners removed from under sentence of death							Under sentence of death, 12/31/98
				Appeal or higher courts overturned					
		Execution	Other death	Death penalty statute	Conviction	Sentence	Sentence commuted	Other or unknown reasons	
1973	42	2	0	14	9	8	9	0	0
1974	149	9	4	65	15	30	22	1	3
1975	298	6	4	171	24	67	21	2	3
1976	233	12	5	136	17	43	15	0	5
1977	137	18	3	40	26	32	7	0	11
1978	187	33	5	21	36	61	8	0	23
1979	152	24	10	2	28	58	5	1	24
1980	174	36	11	3	28	48	7	0	41
1981	229	46	12	0	42	76	4	1	48
1982	268	48	13	0	35	67	7	1	97
1983	254	45	14	1	24	60	6	1	103
1984	283	38	10	2	37	58	6	8	124
1985	268	25	4	1	42	66	4	3	123
1986	299	35	15	0	42	50	6	5	146
1987	289	25	12	4	35	54	2	6	151
1988	291	26	11	0	33	48	3	0	170
1989	263	13	9	0	29	49	3	0	160
1990	252	12	6	0	32	36	1	0	165
1991	264	8	7	0	28	27	3	0	191
1992	289	12	3	0	19	34	3	0	218
1993	291	10	7	0	15	18	3	0	238
1994	321	6	5	0	20	18	1	0	271
1995	322	5	6	0	12	12	0	0	287
1996	317	5	2	0	5	8	0	0	297
1997	274	1	2	0	1	2	0	0	268
1998	285	0	0	0	0	0	0	0	285
Total, 1973-98	6,431	500	180	460	634	1,030	146	29	3,452

Note: For those persons sentenced to death more than once, the numbers are based on the most recent death sentence.

Source: Tracy L. Snell, *Capital Punishment 1998*, Bureau of Justice Statistics, Washington, DC, 1999

the defendant to dispense with the sentence review if the court found him competent to decide for himself (*State v. Torrence*, 473 S.E.2d. 703 [S.C. 1996]). The federal death penalty procedures, on the other hand, did not provide for automatic review after a death sentence was imposed.

While most of the 36 states authorized an automatic review of both conviction and sentence, Idaho, Indiana, Oklahoma, and Tennessee required review of the sentence only. In Idaho, an inmate who wanted his conviction reviewed had to file an appeal or lose his right to do so. In Indiana and Kentucky, a defendant was allowed to waive review of his or her conviction.

The review is usually conducted by the state's highest court of appeals. If the appellate court vacates (annuls) the conviction or the sentence, the case could be returned to the trial court for additional proceedings or for retrial. Subsequent to the resentencing or retrial, the death sentence could be reinstated.

Legal Resources

The Public Defender System

The release of several Illinois inmates, who were found to be innocent (see below) after serving time on death row, has called attention to the nation's public defender system. Death penalty experts claim that some lawyers who defend capital cases are inexperienced and ill-trained. They cite the well-publicized cases of inmates exonerated as a result of college students finding evidence that defense lawyers had failed to uncover. In their November 1999 five-part series, "The Failure of the Death Penalty in Illinois" (*Chicago Tribune*), Ken Armstrong and Steve Mills reported that, at least 33 times, defendants sentenced to death in Illinois had lawyers who were later suspended or disbarred, "sanctions reserved for conduct so incompetent, unethical, or even criminal the lawyer's license [was] taken away."

Some states, such as Colorado and Connecticut, recognizing the complexity in trying capital cases, have put in place capital-case specialists within their public defender offices. Some states, such as Texas, Georgia, and Alabama, have no public defender systems. Judges assign counsel for poor defendants and determine the lawyers' salaries. In most cases, the salary is very low. According to the American Civil Liberties Union (ACLU), defending a capital case takes about 700 to 1,000 hours. Some jurisdictions pay its court-appointed lawyers less than the minimum wage and less than a lawyer's hourly expenses. In addition, courts are not willing to authorize the needed funds for investigating the case and using expert testimony. In contrast, the prosecution usually has unlimited funds at its disposal.

EXECUTING THE INNOCENT

Some people fear that the limitations on federal *habeas corpus* petitions required by the Anti-Terrorism and Effective Death Penalty Act of 1996 (PL 104-132) may facilitate the executions of innocent persons. The act requires death row inmates to file their petitions, in the appropriate district courts, within 180 days of the final denial of their state appeals. Prior to the enactment of this law, there was no filing deadline. Under the 1996 law, a defendant who fails to challenge his or her conviction and sentence within the time specified cannot file another petition unless approved by a three-judge appellate court.

While the overwhelming majority of those sentenced to death are unquestionably guilty of murder, recent exonerations of wrongly convicted persons have caused some legislators, judges, and religious and international leaders to call for a suspension of executions (see Chapter XI). In December 1998, retiring Florida Supreme Court Justice, Gerald Kogan, told the *Washington Post*, "There are several cases where I had grave doubts as to the guilt of a particular person...." First Lady Hillary Rodham Clinton, while continuing to support capital punishment, admitted to being an "unenthusiastic supporter." Former Attorney General of Virginia (1985-86), William G. Broaddus, under whose watch five inmates were executed, is now a death penalty opponent. In 1996, he was co-counsel for Paraguayan Angel Francisco Breard, whose execution caused an international uproar (see Chapter IX).

Since the resumption of the death penalty in 1976, 85 death row inmates have been released (as of February 2000). The average time spent on death row was 7.5 years. Most notable of the persons wrongfully convicted was Anthony Porter of Illinois. Porter came within two days of being executed in September 1998. Questions regarding his mental competency (he has an IQ of 51) prompted the Illinois Supreme Court to stay his execution. Soon after, the collaborative efforts of private investigator Paul Ciolino and Professor David Protess and his investigative journalism students from Northwestern University helped uncover evidence of Porter's innocence. In February 1999, another man confessed to the double murder. On March 11, 1999, Porter's conviction was reversed; he was on death row for 17 years.

Call for Moratorium

In May 1999, the Nebraska legislature approved legislation, setting a two-year moratorium on all executions, pending a study by the Nebraska Crime Commission regarding the application of the death penalty in that state. Although Governor Mike Johanns vetoed the bill, it is believed no executions will occur until the study is completed in December 2000.

Other state legislatures that introduced bills either calling for a moratorium on executions or authorizing studies of the death penalty included Connecticut, Illinois, Maryland, Missouri, Montana, North Carolina, and Pennsylvania. On January 31, 2000, Illinois became the first state to declare a moratorium. Governor George H. Ryan, a death penalty supporter, stated,

> I now favor a moratorium, because I have grave concerns about our state's shameful record of convicting innocent people and putting them on death row. And, I believe, many Illinois residents now feel that same deep reservation. I cannot support a system, which, in its administration, has proven to be so fraught with error and has come so close to the ultimate nightmare, the state's taking of innocent life. Thirteen people have been found to have been wrongfully convicted....

> Until I can be sure that everyone sentenced to death in Illinois is truly guilty, until I can be sure with moral certainty that no innocent man or woman is facing a lethal injection, no one will meet that fate. I am a strong proponent of tough criminal penalties, of supporting laws and programs to help police and prosecutors keep dangerous criminals off the streets. We must ensure the public safety of our citizens but, in doing so, we must ensure that the ends of justice are served.

President Clinton Rejects Calls for a Moratorium

On February 16, 2000, President Bill Clinton announced that he would not impose a national moratorium on the death penalty. Praising Governor George Ryan for suspending executions in Illinois following exonerations of 13 inmates, President Clinton urged other governors to scrutinize their systems of capital punishment. As governor of Arkansas, Clinton had authorized four executions. The President also said the Justice Department is studying whether racial bias plays a role in minorities receiving federal death sentences. Two-thirds of federal death row inmates are minorities.

Innocence Protection Act of 2000

On February 10, 2000, Senator Patrick Leahy (D-VT) introduced the Innocence Protection Act of 2000 (S. 2073) "to reduce the risk that innocent persons may be executed." According to Senator Leahey, in the past decade, based on DNA testing (see below), more than 65 persons in the United States and Canada were found innocent after their convictions. The legislation would ensure that persons wrongfully convicted of any crime would have access to DNA testing and competent counsel. The proposed legislation would require that DNA evidence be preserved for a period of time to permit the defendant to request such evidence to be presented in court. (If properly preserved, DNA samples can be stored indefinitely and tested many years later.)

Furthermore, federal funding would be provided to states that put in place competent legal services for poor defendants in capital cases. In 1996, the Anti-Terrorism and Effective Death Penalty Act (PL 104-132) ended federal funding of regional death penalty resource centers that provided legal services to inmates appealing in federal courts.

DNA Evidence

The National Commission on the Future of DNA Evidence, in *Postconviction DNA Testing: Recommendations for Handling Requests* (National Institute of Justice, Washington, DC, September 1999), observed how, in *Herrara v. Collins* (506 U.S. 390, 1993; see Chapter III), the Supreme Court noted that newly discovered evidence does not constitute grounds for a federal *habeas* relief without showing that a constitutional violation had occurred during state criminal proceedings. Herrera, 10 years after his initial trial, alleged that he was innocent of a double murder, presenting "actual evidence" that his brother, who had since died, had committed the crime. The commission noted that now, with the availability of DNA testing, "the possibility of demonstrating actual innocence has moved from the realm of theory to the actual."

The science of DNA (deoxyribonucleic acid) testing is improving rapidly. DNA technology, not sufficiently developed prior to 1994, has recently played a substantial role in proving the innocence of a number of persons wrongly convicted. Eight of the 85 death row inmates released since 1976 were exonerated by DNA evidence.

When biological material has been left at the scene of the crime, DNA testing could, in some cases, establish with near certainty a defendant's innocence or guilt. DNA, which stores the genetic code of the human body, is found in saliva, skin tissue, bones, blood, semen, and the root and shaft of hair. New sophisticated testings are also able to obtain more accurate information where previous results had proved inconclusive.

In 1996, Professor Protess (see above) and another group of students helped uncover new evidence that proved the innocence of four Black men who were convicted for a 1978 gang rape and double murder. Two received life imprisonment while the other two were sentenced to death. DNA tests helped prove the men's innocence. In March 1999, the four men received a $36 million settlement from Cook County, Illinois, to resolve a lawsuit charging police misconduct.

FAIRNESS AND THE DEATH PENALTY

Racial Questions

Death penalty cases raise a fairness issue. Opponents of the death penalty claim that minorities and poor defendants are more likely to be convicted and receive the death penalty than White and wealthy defendants. In 1987, on appeal, the lawyers for Warren McCleskey, a convicted murderer, brought before the Supreme Court the *Baldus Study* (by Professors David C. Baldus, George Woodworth, and Charles Pulanski), an analysis of 2,000 cases in Georgia in the 1970s. (See Chapter IV.)

This study showed that Black defendants who were convicted of killing Whites were more likely to receive death sentences than White murderers or than Blacks who killed Black victims. The justices, in *McCleskey v. Kemp* (481 U.S. 279, 1987), rejected the study, declaring that "apparent disparities ... are an inevitable part of our criminal justice system" and that there were enough safeguards built into the legal system to protect every defendant.

In 1998, Dr. Davis Baldus et al., expanding on the *Baldus Study,* found evidence of race-of-victim disparities in 26 out of 29 death penalty states. ("Racial Discrimination and the Death Penalty in the Post-*Furman* Era: An Empirical and Legal Analysis with Recent Findings from Philadelphia," 83 *Cornell Law Review* 1661). The researchers found that the race of the victim was related to whether capital punishment was imposed. A defendant was more likely to receive the death penalty if the victim was White than if the victim was Black.

These studies were consistent with a 1990 U.S. government study of capital punishment. The U.S. General Accounting Office (GAO), in *Death Penalty Sentencing: Research Indicates Pattern of Racial Disparities* (Washington, DC), reviewed 28 studies on race and the death penalty. The GAO reported that "in 82 percent of the studies, the race of the victim was found to influence the likelihood of being charged with capital murder or receiving the death penalty." The GAO found that when the victim was White, the defendant, whether White or Black, was more likely to get the death sentence.

The studies also showed that for crimes of passion, the convicted person rarely received the death penalty. Moreover, in the small number of horrendous murders, death sentences were more likely to be imposed, regardless of race. However, when the offender killed a person while robbing him or when the murderer had a previous record, the race of the victim played a role.

In September 1999, in his testimony before the Illinois House of Representatives' hearing on the state's system of capital punishment, Richard C. Dieter, executive director of the Death Penalty Information Center, which supports the abolition of capital punishment, noted,

> Ten out of 12 people who have been released from Illinois's death row are members of a minority. Most are African American. That doesn't prove bias, but it should raise concerns. Illinois's death row is made up of approximately 156 individuals, 97 of whom are Black — that's 62 percent in a state where the Black population is less than 15 percent. Again, those figures do not prove any racial bias, but such a glaring disproportion is evidence that something is wrong at some level of society. If race is playing a role in who is sentenced to death, then it can also be playing a role in who is wrongly convicted.

Some persons claim that district attorneys, who alone decide which case to try as a death penalty case, may be motivated by politics or racial prejudice to impose the death penalty on a minority. Professor Jeffrey Pokorak of St. Mary's University School of Law, in "Probing the Capital Prosecutor's Perspective: Race of the Discretionary Actors" (83 *Cornell Law Review* 1811 [1998]), found that 97.5 percent (1,794 out of 1,838 prosecutors in the 38 states with capital punishment) were White. Only 1.2 percent each were Black and Hispanic.

Legislation

In 1998, Kentucky became the first state to enact a racial justice law, prohibiting the execution of a convicted person when evidence shows racial discrimination in prosecution or sentencing. Other states that have considered a similar legislation included Florida, Indiana, Nebraska, New Mexico, North Carolina, Ohio, Oregon, and Texas.

THE COSTS OF EXECUTIONS

Most death penalty opponents advocate life imprisonment without the chance of parole as an alternative to the death sentence. Some people, however, believe that capital punishment costs the taxpayers less than paying for the expenses of an inmate who is incarcerated for life. Several studies of capital punishment have found that it costs more than life imprisonment without parole. Hugo Adam Bedau, in *The Case Against the Death Penalty* (American Civil Liberties Union, Washington, DC, 1997), found that "[a] murder trial normally takes longer when the death penalty is at issue than when it is not. Litigation costs — including the time of judges, prosecutors, public defenders, and court reporters, and the high costs of briefs — are mostly borne by the taxpayer."

Various Estimates

North Carolina

Phillip J. Cook and Donna B. Slawson, professors of public policy at Duke University, in *The Costs of Processing Murder Cases in North Carolina* (1993), studied the total costs of every death penalty case in the state for over two years. They found that in North Carolina, the cost to try a noncapital murder case and imprison a convicted murderer for 20 years was $166,000. The cost to try a capital murder case, convict, and execute a prisoner after 10 years of imprisonment averaged $329,000. A noncapital murder case thus saved the state and local governments an estimated $163,000.

However, only one-third (31 percent) of the capital murder trials resulted in a sentence of death. Only about 10 percent of those condemned to death were actually executed. Many of those sentenced to death had retrials or new sentencing trials, which had different results than their original trials. Cook and Slawson estimated that the extra cost for each case in which the defendant was sentenced to death was about $216,000. The extra cost per case in which the defendant was executed was more than $2.16 million.

Some of the costs incurred in a capital murder case — providing indigent defendants with two lawyers instead of one (which is their right), calling more expert witnesses, and filing more briefs — might not have been incurred in a noncapital murder trial in North Carolina. The appeals process had nine steps, some of which could be repeated.

New York

The state of New York established the Capital Defender Office upon the reinstatement of the death penalty in 1995. The state allocates about $15 million annually for capital defense expenses. As of December 1999, out of nearly 500 defendants charged with first-degree murder or the possibility of first-degree murder since 1995, New York prosecutors sought the death penalty in 37 cases. The nine death penalty cases tried so far resulted in five death sentences and four life imprisonments without parole.

No system is in place to track prosecution costs because district attorneys employ different methods to do so. Experts estimate that the prosecution costs probably equal, or exceed, that of defense expenses. Since death penalty cases often drag on for years, by the time the death row inmate is executed, the cost is tenfold. (In 1998, the 68 inmates who were executed nationwide were under sentence of death for an average of 10 years and 10 months. See Table 7.10.)

California

A study of the California system suggested a minimum cost of $500,000 per case (this included all capital cases, not just the ones that ended with a death sentence). In 1994, California set up the Office of Public Defender, which works exclusively on appeals for poor defendants on death row at an annual cost of $8 million. Because the office cannot handle all the defendants, the state offers private attorneys contracts for $75,000

to $200,000 to handle cases. Despite these efforts, about one-third of the prisoners on death row do not have lawyers to represent them in the appeals process. Many death penalty cases are on hold because lawyers cannot be found to handle the appeals.

Federal Death Penalty Costs

Since the passage of the Violent Crime Control and Law Enforcement Act (PL 103-322; also known as the Federal Death Penalty Act of 1994), the number of federal prosecutions, including crimes punishable by death, has risen. The Subcommittee on Federal Death Penalty Cases of the Committee on Defender Services of the Judicial Conference of the United States, in *Federal Death Penalty Cases: Recommendations Concerning the Cost and Quality of Defense Representation* (Washington, DC, 1998), estimated that about 560 federal death penalty cases were filed between 1991 and 1997, increasing from 12 cases in 1991, rising nearly tenfold to 118 in 1995 and reaching 153 cases in 1997 (Figure 7.2).

Although the decision to charge a crime punishable by death is made by the local federal prosecutor, the U.S. Attorney General alone authorizes

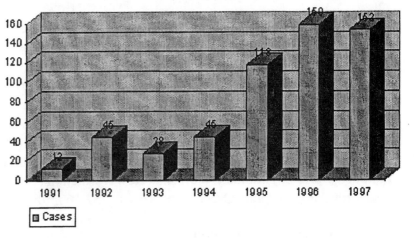

FIGURE 7.2

Federal Death Penalty Cases By Year of Indictment

Source: *Federal Death Penalty Cases: Recommendations Concerning the Cost and Quality of Defense Representation*, Subcommittee on Federal Death Penalty Cases, Committee on Defender Services, Judicial Conference of the United States, Washington, DC, 1998

TABLE 7.13

Average Number of Attorney Hours Billed in

Capital and Non-Capital Homicide Cases

	Case Type	In Court Hours	Out of Court Hours	Avg. Total Attorney Hours Per Representation
Non-Capital	Homicides	18	100	117
Capital	Auth. Denied	38	391	429
	Auth. Granted	231	1,233	1,464
	Capital Trial	409	1,480	1,889
	Plea	61	1,201	1,262
	Drug Cases	277	1,343	1,619

Source: *Federal Death Penalty Cases: Recommendations Concerning the Cost and Quality of Defense Representation*, Subcommittee on Federal Death Penalty Cases, Committee on Defender Services, Judicial Conference of the United States, Washington, DC, 1998

the seeking of the death penalty. Between 1988 and December 1997, the U.S. Attorney General authorized seeking capital punishment in 111 cases. The Attorney General's decision to authorize seeking the death penalty makes a substantial difference in the cost of representing a defendant. From 1990 to 1997, the average total cost (for counsel and related services) per representation of a sample of cases in which the defendant was charged with an offense punishable by death and the Attorney General authorized seeking the death penalty (includes cases resolved by a guilty plea as well as cases resolved by a trial) was $218,112. In contrast, the average total cost per representation in which the defendant was charged with an offense punishable by death and the Attorney General did not authorize seeking the death penalty was $55,772.

The decision whether to go to trial or to enter a guilty plea also affects the cost of representing the alleged offender. Between 1988 and 1997, of the 111 cases in which the Attorney General sought the death sentence, 41 were tried for capital charges. Cases that ended in capital trials cost an average of $269,139, compared to $192,333 for cases resolved with a guilty plea.

Since a death penalty case differs from other cases in that a defendant's life is at stake, the defense generally devotes more time to the case. One time-consuming aspect of the defense involves prolonged jury selection. While jury selection in noncapital cases may take a couple of days, in capital cases, it may take several months. Table 7.13 shows the difference in the number of billable hours in capital and noncapital homicide cases as compiled by the Subcommittee on Federal Death Penalty Cases (see above).

Those who support capital punishment, however, believe that the issue of justice should not be based upon cost. It might be more expensive to guarantee fairness to both the alleged perpetrator and the victim, but the cost is justified if the fair handling of the case is achieved.

73

Intangible Costs

The cost of imposing the death penalty can also be counted in ways other than dollars. A Texas spokesperson for VOTERS (Victims Organized to Ensure Rights and Safety) commented that only in rare cases does the organization support the death penalty over life without parole. Because the process is so long and difficult, the family of the murder victim is required to relive their nightmare many times at each appeal, each hearing, and each scheduled execution date. In 1998, John Weiler of Florida, who waited 17 years while Allen Lee Davis (see Chapter V) appealed his case in the brutal murder of Weiler's pregnant wife and two young daughters, said, "It is cruel and unusual punishment of the victims, living and dead, to know that this animal ... still breathes."

CHAPTER VIII

PUBLIC ATTITUDES TOWARD CAPITAL PUNISHMENT*

Most Americans strongly favor capital punishment. In 1999, the Harris Poll (Table 8.1) and the Gallup Organization (Table 8.2) found that 7 in 10 (71 percent) Americans supported the death penalty. A 1998 survey by the National Opinion Research Center showed a similar finding — 67 percent of Americans favored capital punishment for murder convictions, while 24 percent opposed it (Table 8.3).

SUPPORT INCREASING

Over the past three decades, the Harris Poll has reported an increase in support for capital punishment. In 1965, two years before a death penalty moratorium (temporary suspension) occurred, almost two-fifths (38 percent) of the population believed in the im-

position of the death penalty. By 1976, when the death penalty was reinstated, the proportion of Americans favoring the death penalty rose to 67

TABLE 8.1

BELIEVE IN CAPITAL PUNISHMENT

"Do you believe in capital punishment, that is the death penalty, or are you opposed to it?"

	1965 %	1969 %	1970 %	1973 %	1976 %	1983 %	1997 %	1999 %
Believe in it	38	48	47	59	67	68	75	71
Opposed	47	38	42	31	25	27	22	21
Not sure/Refused	15	14	11	10	8	5	3	8

Source: Harris Poll #45, Harris Interactive, New York, NY, 1999

TABLE 8.2

Are you in favor of the death penalty for a person convicted of murder? (Based on 543 national adult: margin of error plus or minus 5 percentage points)

	For	Against	No Opinion
99 Feb 8-9	71%	22%	7%

Source: The Gallup Organization, Princeton, NJ, 1999

---

* Like all statistics, public opinion polls should be viewed cautiously. The way a question is phrased influences the respondents' answers. Many other factors may also influence a response in ways that are often difficult to determine. A respondent might never have thought of the issue until asked, or he/she might be giving the pollster the answer he/she thinks the pollster wants to hear. Organizations that survey opinions do not claim absolute accuracy — their findings are approximate snapshots of the attitudes of the nation at a given time. The surveys presented here have been selected from numerous polls taken on capital punishment. The Gallup Organization, Harris Interactive (formerly Louis Harris and Associates, Inc.), and the National Opinion Research Center are well respected in their fields, and their surveys are accepted as representative of public opinions. A typical, well-conducted survey claims accuracy to about plus or minus three points.

percent. The support for the death penalty peaked in 1997, with 3 out of 4 Americans (75 percent) favoring it and only 1 out of 5 (22 percent) opposing it. (See Table 8.1.)

In 1999, support for capital punishment dropped somewhat to 71 percent. The Harris Poll researchers believe this may have been due to the well-publicized cases of wrongful convictions. In several cases, DNA evidence has helped exonerate innocent people who had been sentenced to death. (See Chapter VII.)

Men (75 percent) were more likely than women (66 percent) to support capital punishment. Whites (77 percent) tended to favor the death penalty more than Hispanics (65 percent) and Blacks (39 percent). Republicans (81 percent) were more likely than Independents (75 percent) and Democrats (64 percent) to believe in the death penalty. (See Table 8.4.)

The percentage of those believing in the death penalty increased with age (with the exception of people 65 and over) and income. The support for the death penalty varied with the degree of education, with those having a postgraduate degree favoring it the least. People living in the South were the most likely to favor the death penalty. (See Table 8.4.)

ACCEPTABLE PENALTY FOR MURDER

In 1936, the first time the Gallup Organization polled Americans regarding their attitudes toward the death penalty for murder, 3 in 5 (61 percent) respondents favored the death penalty. For nearly 40 years, support for capital punishment fluctuated. Starting in 1971, support for capital punishment steadily increased, peaking at 80 percent in 1994. By 1999, support for capital punishment dropped to 71 percent, with one-quarter (22 percent) of Americans opposing it. (See Tables 8.2 and 8.5.)

The lowest proportion to support capital punishment for murder was 42 percent in 1966, a period of civil rights and anti-Vietnam War marches,

TABLE 8.3

Do you favor or oppose the death penalty for persons convicted of murder?

	Favor %	Oppose %	Don't Know %
1972-82	66	28	---
1983-87	72	22	5
1988-91	72	21	6
1993	72	21	7
1994	74	19	6
1996	71	21	7
1998	67	24	7

Source: National Opinion Research Center, University of Chicago, IL, 1999; table constructed by Information Plus

"flower children," and the peace movement. It was also the only time in the 63 years (as of 1999) of Gallup polling that those who opposed capital punishment (47 percent) outnumbered those who favored it (42 percent). (See Table 8.5.)

Death Penalty vs. Life Imprisonment with No Parole

Most people sentenced to life imprisonment are likely to get out on parole at some time in the future. Some people point to this as their reason for favoring the death penalty. In 1999, when the Gallup Poll asked whether the penalty for murder should be execution or life imprisonment with no possibility of parole, support for the death penalty dropped to 56 percent, with 38 percent of respondents favoring a life sentence without parole. (See Table 8.6.) Apparently, a substantial proportion of people who supported the death penalty would advocate life imprisonment if they could be guaranteed the killer would never get out of prison.

In 1998, the Gallup Poll asked the same question, indicating the gender of the criminal offender. An almost equal proportion (54 percent for male

TABLE 8.4

Attitudes toward the death penalty

By demographic characteristics, United States, 1999[a]

Question: "Do you believe in capital punishment, that is, the death penalty, or are you opposed to it?"

	Believe in it	Opposed to it	Not sure/ refused
National	71%	21%	8%
Sex			
Male	75	20	5
Female	66	23	11
Race, ethnicity			
White	77	15	8
Black	39	51	10
Hispanic	65	32	3
Age			
18 to 24 years	59	33	9
25 to 29 years	69	22	10
30 to 39 years	71	21	8
40 to 49 years	73	17	9
50 to 64 years	78	18	4
65 years and older	71	22	7
Education			
College post graduate	59	34	6
College graduate	74	20	5
Some college	71	23	6
Less than college	72	19	9
Income			
Over $75,000	75	18	7
$50,001 to $75,000	72	21	7
$35,001 to $50,000	74	21	5
$25,001 to $35,000	72	21	7
$15,001 to $25,000	68	25	7
$15,000 or less	68	20	13
Region			
East	67	28	5
Midwest	70	20	9
South	74	17	9
West	71	23	7
Politics			
Republican	81	12	8
Democrat	64	28	8
Independent	75	19	6

[a]Percents may not add to 100 because of rounding.

Source: Kathleen Maguire and Ann L. Pastore, eds., *Sourcebook of Criminal Justice Statistics 1998*, Bureau of Justice Statistics, Washington, DC, 1999

TABLE 8.5

DEATH PENALTY FOR MURDER TREND

	Yes	No
1936	61	39
1937	65	35
1953	68	25
1960	51	36
1965	45	43
1966	42	47
1969	51	40
1971	49	40
1972	57	32
1976	65	28
1978	62	27
1981	66	25
1985	72	20
1986*	70	22
1988*	79	16
1991	76	18
1994	80	16
1995	77	13
1996	79	18

* "Do you favor or oppose ..."

Note: "No Opinion" omitted

Source: The Gallup Organization, Princeton, NJ, 1996

offenders and 50 percent for females) of respondents thought capital punishment should be the penalty for murder. Similar percentages (36 percent for male offenders and 38 for females) of respondents chose life imprisonment with no possibility of parole. (See Table 8.7.)

SUPPORT FOR CAPITAL PUNISHMENT IS LOWER IN SPECIFIC CASES

Although most Americans generally favor the death penalty, they tend to be more lenient when a survey mentions a specific offender. In August 1999, after Buford Furrow killed a postal carrier during a shooting spree in a Jewish community center in Los Angeles, a CNN/*USA Today*/Gallup Poll survey found that 55 percent of the American public favored the death penalty for Furrow if he were convicted. This figure is 16 percentage points lower than the 71 percent general support for capital punishment that same year.

In 1998, a *Dallas Morning News* survey found that, although most (75 percent) Texans generally favored capital punishment, less than half (45 percent) supported the death penalty for Karla Faye Tucker, the second woman to be executed since the reinstatement of the death penalty in 1976. In

TABLE 8.6

What do you think should be the penalty for murder—the death penalty, or life imprisonment with absolutely no possibility of parole? (Based on 511 national adult: margin of error plus or minus 5 percentage points)

	Death Penalty	Life Imprisonment	No Opinion
99 Feb 8-9	56%	38%	6%

Source: The Gallup Organization, Princeton, NJ, 1999

TABLE 8.7

(Asked of Form A) On another subject, what do you think should be the penalty for murder committed by a *man* — the death penalty, or life imprisonment with absolutely no possibility of parole?

Death penalty	54%
Life imprisonment	36
Other/neither (vol.)	5
No opinion	5
	100%

(Asked of Form B) What do you think should be the penalty for murder committed by a *woman* — the death penalty, or life imprisonment with absolutely no possibility of parole?

Death penalty	50%
Life imprisonment	38
Other/neither (vol.)	7
No opinion	5
	100%

Source: *The Gallup Poll Monthly*, January 1998

TABLE 8.8

In your opinion, is the death penalty imposed too often today or not enough?

	Too Often	Not Often Enough	About the Right Amount	No Opinion
99 Feb 8-9	25%	64%	4%	7%

Source: The Gallup Organization, Princeton, NJ, 1999

1997, after Oklahoma City bomber, Timothy McVeigh, was convicted, one-third (34 percent) of Gallup Poll respondents supported life imprisonment without the possibility of parole, compared to two-thirds (64 percent) favoring capital punishment.

IS THE DEATH PENALTY IMPOSED TOO OFTEN?

Interestingly, although the United States leads all Western countries in executions, just one-quarter (25 percent) of Americans surveyed by the

Gallup Organization in 1999 felt the death penalty is imposed too often. Two-thirds (64 percent) thought it is not used often enough, while just 4 percent thought the level of death-penalty imposition is about right. (See Table 8.8.)

The Gallup Poll also found that non-Whites were more likely to oppose the death penalty than Whites. Two in 5 (41 percent) non-Whites believed the death penalty is imposed too often, while 1 in 5 (22 percent) Whites thought so. In contrast, two-thirds (66 percent) of Whites indicated the death penalty is not used enough, while half (52 percent) of non-Whites said so.

DEATH PENALTY FAVORED
EVEN IF SOME ARE INNOCENT

The Death Penalty Information Center (Washington, DC), a nonprofit organization that opposes capital punishment, reports that, since 1973, 85 inmates (as of January 25, 2000) have been released from death row after proof of innocence. The Center attributes the discovery of mistaken convictions to DNA tests, research by journalism students and reporters, and volunteer legal work "outside of the normal appeals process." (See Chapter VII.)

In 1999, the Harris Poll found that virtually all Americans (95 percent) believed that, on average, for every 100 people convicted of murder, 1 in 9 (11 percent) are innocent. Women guessed that this occurs more often (estimate of 13 percent) than men did (8 percent). Blacks estimated that 18 percent of people convicted of murder are innocent, compared to estimates by Hispanics (11 percent) and Whites (10 percent). Democrats and those with a high school degree or less were more likely to believe that a higher proportion of innocent people are convicted of murder. Supporters of the death

---

TABLE 8.9

WHAT PERCENT OF PEOPLE CONVICTED OF MURDER ARE INNOCENT?

Base: Innocent people are sometimes convicted of murder (95%)

"For every one hundred people convicted of murder, how many would you guess are actually innocent?"

	Mean Estimate
All Adults	11%
Sex	
Men	8%
Women	13%
Race/Ethnicity	
White	10%
African-American	18%
Hispanic	11%
Education	
High school or less	13%
Some college	9%
College graduate	6%
Post graduate	7%
Party	
Republican	7%
Democrat	12%
Independent	8%
Support for Death Penalty	
Believe in it	8%
Oppose it	15%

Source: Harris Poll #45, Harris Interactive, New York, NY, 1999

TABLE 8.10

IS CAPITAL PUNSHIMENT A DETERRENT?

"Do you feel that executing people who commit murder deters others from committing murder, or do you think such executions don't have much effect?"

	1976 %	1983 %	1997 %	1999 %
Deters others	59	63	49	47
Not much effect	34	32	49	49
Not sure/Refused	7	5	2	4

Source: Harris Poll #45, Harris Interactive, New York, NY, 1999

penalty gave a lower estimate (8 percent) of the percentage of people wrongfully convicted. (See Table 8.9.)

Of the 95 percent of respondents who indicated they believed a "substantial number" of innocent people are convicted of murder, half (51 percent) would oppose the death penalty, and 38 percent would support it.

CRIMES DESERVING
THE DEATH PENALTY

In 1997, a *Time*/CNN poll found that 74 percent of the public favored the death penalty for persons convicted of serious crimes, with only 20 percent opposing it. Seventy-eight percent wanted the death penalty imposed on a person guilty of presidential assassination, and 75 percent favored capital punishment for a murder of a police officer or of an ordinary citizen. In addition, the death penalty was favored by 65 percent for child molestation, 47 percent for rape, and 44 percent for selling drugs to children.

DETERRENT OR NOT?

A 1999 Harris Poll found that Americans were split between those who felt that capital punishment deters (discourages) people from committing murders (47 percent) and those who believed capital punishment has no such effect (49 percent). In 1976, when the death penalty was reinstated, 3 in 5 (59 percent) Americans thought capital punishment was a deterrent, compared to 3 in 10 (34 percent) who thought it was not a deterrent. (See Table 8.10.)

Interestingly, the same 1999 Harris Poll found that 43 percent of Americans favored an increase in the number of executions, 21 percent favored a decrease, and 28 percent favored no change. In 1997, over half (53 percent) of the public favored an increase in the use of the death penalty, 14 percent favored a decrease, and the same proportion (27 percent) wanted no change.

CHAPTER IX

CAPITAL PUNISHMENT AROUND THE WORLD

UNITED NATIONS RESOLUTIONS

Capital punishment is controversial not only in the United States but also in many other countries of the world. The ethical arguments that fuel the debate in the United States also characterize the discussion in other countries. The United Nations' position on capital punishment is a compromise among those countries that want it completely abolished, those that want it limited to very serious offenses, and those that want it left up to each country to decide. In 1957, after 11 years of debate, a statement on the death penalty was included in the International Covenant on Civil and Political Rights, which the General Assembly adopted in Resolution 2200 (XXI) of December 16, 1966. Article 6 of the Covenant states,

• Every human being has the inherent right to life. This right shall be protected by law. No one shall be arbitrarily deprived of his life.

• In countries that have not abolished the death penalty, sentence of death may be imposed only for the most serious crimes in accordance with the law in force at the time of the commission of the crime and not contrary to the provisions of the present Covenant and to the Convention on the Prevention and Punishment of the Crime of Genocide (systematic killing of a racial, political, or cultural group). This penalty can only be carried out pursuant to a final judgment rendered by a competent court.

• When deprivation of life constitutes the crime of genocide, it is understood that nothing in this article shall authorize any State Party to the present Covenant to derogate (turn away) in any way from any obligation assumed under the provisions of the Convention on the Prevention and Punishment of the Crime of Genocide.

• Anyone sentenced to death shall have the right to seek pardon or commutation of the sentence. Amnesty, pardon, or commutation of the sentence of death may be granted in all cases.

• Sentence of death shall not be imposed for crimes committed by persons below eighteen years of age and shall not be carried out on pregnant women.

• Nothing in this article shall be invoked to delay or prevent the abolition of capital punishment by any State Party to the present Covenant.

The United Nations (UN) has dealt with the death penalty in several other documents and meetings. Among them is General Assembly Resolution 2393 (XXIII) of November 26, 1968, which specifies the following legal safeguards that should be offered condemned prisoners by countries with capital punishment:

• A person condemned to death shall not be deprived of the right to appeal to a higher judicial authority or, as the case may be, to petition for pardon or reprieve (postponement or cancellation of punishment).

• A death sentence shall not be carried out until the procedures of appeal or, as the case may be, of petition for pardon or reprieve have been terminated.

TABLE 9.1

RETENTIONIST

AFGHANISTAN
ALGERIA
ANTIGUA AND BARBUDA
ARMENIA
BAHAMAS
BAHRAIN
BANGLADESH
BARBADOS
BELARUS
BELIZE
BENIN
BOTSWANA
BURKINA FASO
BURUNDI
CAMEROON
CHAD
CHILE
CHINA
COMOROS
CONGO (Democratic Republic)
CUBA
DOMINICA
EGYPT
EQUATORIAL GUINEA
ERITREA
ETHIOPIA
GABON
GHANA
GUATEMALA
GUINEA
GUYANA
INDIA
INDONESIA
IRAN
IRAQ
JAMAICA
JAPAN
JORDAN
KAZAKSTAN
KENYA
KUWAIT
KYRGYZSTAN
LAOS
LEBANON
LESOTHO
LIBERIA
LIBYA
MALAWI
MALAYSIA
MAURITANIA
MONGOLIA

MOROCCO
MYANMAR
NIGERIA
NORTH KOREA
OMAN
PAKISTAN
PALESTINIAN AUTHORITY
PHILIPPINES
QATAR
RUSSIAN FEDERATION
RWANDA
SAINT CHRISTOPHER AND NEVIS
SAINT LUCIA
SAINT VINCENT AND GRENADINES
SAUDI ARABIA
SIERRA LEONE
SINGAPORE
SOMALIA
SOUTH KOREA
SUDAN
SWAZILAND
SYRIA
TAIWAN
TAJIKISTAN
TANZANIA
THAILAND
TRINIDAD AND TOBAGO
TUNISIA
TURKMENISTAN
UGANDA
UKRAINE
UNITED ARAB EMIRATES
UNITED STATES OF AMERICA
UZBEKISTAN
VIET NAM
YEMEN
YUGOSLAVIA (Federal Republic)
ZAMBIA
ZIMBABWE

Source: *The Death Penalty: List of Abolitionist and Retentionist Countries*, 1999, © Amnesty International Publications, 1 Easton Street, London WC1X 0DJ, United Kingdom, www.amnesty.org

- Special attention shall be given in the case of indigent (poor) persons by the provision of adequate legal assistance at all stages of the proceedings.

Since then, the UN has come out more strongly for eliminating capital punishment. General Assembly Resolution 2857 (XXVI) of December 20, 1971, observed,

> In order to guarantee fully the right to life, provided for in Article 3 of the Universal Declaration of Human Rights, the main objective to be pursued is that of progressively restricting the number of offenses for which capital punishment may be imposed, with a view to the desirability of abolishing this punishment in all countries.

The UN Economic and Social Council Resolution 1574 (L) of May 20, 1971, made a similar declaration. In 1984, the Economic and Social Council adopted the *Safeguards Guaranteeing Protection of the Rights of Those Facing the Death Penalty*, including persons younger than age 18 at the time the crime was committed. Subsequently, over the years, General Assembly and Economic and Social Council resolutions have called for the eventual abolition of the death penalty.

Recent United Nations Initiatives

On April 28, 1999, the UN Commission on Human Rights voted 30-11, with 12 abstentions, in favor of a worldwide moratorium on executions. The resolution was sponsored by the European Union. The United States and China, considered the most frequent users of the death penalty, voted against the moratorium. The other nine countries opposing the moratorium were Bangladesh, Botswana, Indonesia, Japan, Pakistan, Rwanda, South Korea, Sudan, and Qatar.

On August 24, 1999, the UN Sub-Commission on the Promotion and Protection of Human Rights

- Call[ed] upon all states which retain the death penalty and do not apply a moratorium on executions, in order to mark the millennium, to commute the sentences of those under sentence of death on 31 December 1999 at least to sentences of life imprisonment and to commit themselves to a moratorium on the imposition of the death penalty throughout the year 2000.

- [For the first time in a UN resolution], call[ed] upon all states that retain the death penalty for refusal to undertake military services or for desertion not to apply the death penalty where the refusal to undertake military service or the desertion is the result of conscientious objection to such service.

RETENTIONIST COUNTRIES

Amnesty International (AI), a human rights organization headquartered in London, United Kingdom, maintains information on capital punishment throughout the world. (AI vehemently opposes the death penalty, considering it the "ultimate form of cruel, inhuman, and degrading punishment.") The organization refers to countries that retain and use the death penalty as retentionist countries; those that no longer use the death penalty are known as abolitionist countries.

As of December 18, 1999, 90 countries and territories in the world retained and used the death penalty as a possible punishment for ordinary crimes.* (See Table 9.1.) Although many of these retentionist countries had not executed anybody in many years, a small number of countries continues to carry out numerous executions.

---

* "Ordinary" crimes are crimes committed during peacetime. Ordinary crimes that could lead to the death penalty include murder, rape, and, in some countries, robbery or embezzlement of very large sums of money. "Exceptional" crimes are military crimes or crimes committed during exceptional times, mainly wartime. Examples are treason, spying, or desertion (leaving the armed services without permission).

AI reports that, in 1998, four countries accounted for 86 percent of executions worldwide — China (1,700), the Democratic Republic of Congo (100), the United States (68), and Iran (66). Iraq reportedly put many people to death, but AI had not been able to determine the exact count.

In 1998, 2,258 reported executions occurred in 37 countries. Another 78 countries sentenced 4,845 people to death. Amnesty International believes that the actual numbers of those executed and sentenced to death were much higher than cases known to the organization.

United States

The United States remains the only Western country that practices capital punishment. (The federal government and 38 states have the death penalty.) In September 1997, for the first time, a United Nations monitor investigated the use of the death penalty in the United States. In his report to

TABLE 9.2

ABOLITIONIST DE FACTO

Abbreviations: **Date (last ex.)** = date of last execution; **K** = date of last known execution; **Ind.** = no executions since independence

Country	Date of Last Execution
ALBANIA	
BERMUDA*	1977
BHUTAN	1964 K
BRUNEI DARUSSALAM	1957 K
CENTRAL AFRICAN REPUBLIC	1981
CONGO (Republic)	1982
COTE D'IVOIRE	
DJIBOUTI	Ind.
GAMBIA	1981
GRENADA	1978
MADAGASCAR	1958 K
MALDIVES	1952 K
MALI	1980
NAURU	Ind.
NIGER	1976 K
PAPUA NEW GUINEA	1950
SENEGAL	1967
SRI LANKA	1976
SURINAME	1982
TOGO	
TONGA	1982
TURKEY	1984
WESTERN SAMOA	Ind.

* On December 23, 1999, Bermuda abolished the death penalty for all crimes.

Source: *The Death Penalty: List of Abolitionist and Retentionist Countries*, 1999, © Amnesty International Publications, 1 Easton Street, London WC1X 0DJ, United Kingdom, www.amnesty.org

the United Nations Commission on Human Rights, the special investigator accused the United States of unfair, arbitrary, and racist use of capital punishment. He claimed that "allegations of racial discrimination in the imposition of death sentences are particularly serious in southern states, such as Alabama, Florida, Louisiana, Mississippi, Georgia and Texas, known as the 'death penalty belt.'"

Foreign Nationals

As of January 1, 2000, about 80 foreign nationals were on death row in the United States. Capital punishment opponents claim that the United States generally does not inform foreign nationals under arrest that they have the right to consult with the consulate of their home country as required by Article 36 of the Vienna Convention on Consular Relations. The United States has ratified this international agreement. In 1999, the United States executed five foreign nationals.

The United States Defies UN's Highest Court

In November 1999, the United States formally apologized to Paraguay for failing to inform Angel Francisco Breard, a Paraguayan national, of his right to seek consular assistance after his arrest on capital murder charges in 1992. Breard was executed on April 14, 1998, despite requests for a stay of execution from Secretary of State Madeleine Albright, the Paraguayan government, and the International Court of Justice (UN's highest judicial organ).

In 1993, Breard was sentenced to death after his convictions for rape and capital murder. Following the denial of his appeals before the Virginia Supreme Court and the U.S. Supreme Court, Breard invoked the provision of the Vienna Convention on Consular Relations (see above). The U.S. District Court, in *Breard v. Netherland* (945 F. Supp. 1255, 1266 [ED Va. 1996]), rejected Breard's claim because he had "procedurally defaulted" the claim when he failed to raise it in state court. In addition, the district court concluded that Breard could not show cause and prejudice for this default.

At the same time, in 1996, the Republic of Paraguay brought suit against Virginia officials for violation of the Vienna Convention because it failed to notify the Paraguayan consulate of Breard's arrest. The district court dismissed the suit, which the appellate court affirmed. On April 3, 1998, the Republic of Paraguay brought the case before the International Court of Justice (ICJ), which ruled, on April 9, 1998, that the United States should stay Breard's execution pending ICJ's final decision. Paraguay had also petitioned the U.S. Supreme Court.

On the day of the execution, the U.S. Supreme Court, in *Paraguay et al. v. Gilmore* (No. 97-1390 [S-738]), refused to intervene in the case. The Court stated,

> It is the rule in this country that assertions of error in criminal proceedings must first be raised in state court in order to form the basis for relief in habeas.... Claims not so raised are considered defaulted. By not asserting his Vienna Convention claim in state court, Breard failed to exercise his rights under the Vienna Convention in conformity with the laws of the United States and the Commonwealth of Virginia. Having failed to do so, he cannot raise a claim of violation of those rights now on federal habeas review.

> As for Paraguay's suits (both the original action and the case coming to us on petition for certiorari), neither the text nor the history of the Vienna Convention clearly provides a foreign nation a private right of action in United States courts to set aside a criminal conviction and sentence for violation of consular notification provisions.... Though Paraguay claims that its suit is within an exemption dealing with continuing consequences of past violations of federal rights, we do not agree. The failure to notify the Paraguayan Consul occurred long ago and has no continuing effect....

TABLE 9.3
ABOLITIONIST FOR ALL CRIMES

Abbreviations: **Date (A)** = date of abolition for all crimes; **Date (AO)** = date of abolition for ordinary crimes; **Date (last ex.)** = date of last execution; **K** = date of last known execution; **Ind.** = no executions since independence

Country	Date (A)	Date (AO)	Date (last ex.)
ANDORRA	1990		1943
ANGOLA	1992		
AUSTRALIA	1985	1984	1967
AUSTRIA	1968	1950	1950
AZERBAIJAN	1998		1993
BELGIUM	1996		1950
BULGARIA	1998		1989
CAMBODIA	1989		
CANADA	1998	1976	1962
CAPE VERDE	1981		1835
COLOMBIA	1910		1909
COSTA RICA	1877		
CROATIA	1990		
CZECH REPUBLIC	1990		
DENMARK	1978	1933	1950
DOMINICAN REPUBLIC	1966		
EAST TIMOR	1999		
ECUADOR	1906		
ESTONIA	1998		1991
FINLAND	1972	1949	1944
FRANCE	1981		1977
GEORGIA	1997		1994 K
GERMANY	1987		
GREECE	1993		1972
GUINEA-BISSAU	1993		1986 K
HAITI	1987		1972 K
HONDURAS	1956		1940
HUNGARY	1990		1988
ICELAND	1928		1830
IRELAND	1990		1954
ITALY	1994	1947	1947
KIRIBATI			Ind.
LIECHTENSTEIN	1987		1785
LITHUANIA	1998		1995
LUXEMBOURG	1979		1949
MACEDONIA (former Yug. Rep.)			
MARSHALL ISLANDS			Ind.

(continued)

TABLE 9.3 (Continued)

MAURITIUS	1995		1987
MICRONESIA (Federated States)			Ind.
MOLDOVA	1995		
MONACO	1962		1847
MOZAMBIQUE	1990		1986
NAMIBIA	1990		1988 K
NEPAL	1997	1990	1979
NETHERLANDS	1982	1870	1952
NEW ZEALAND	1989	1961	1957
NICARAGUA	1979		1930
NORWAY	1979	1905	1948
PALAU			
PANAMA			1903 K
PARAGUAY	1992		1928
POLAND	1997		1988
PORTUGAL	1976	1867	1849 K
ROMANIA	1989		1989
SAN MARINO	1865	1848	1468 K
SÃO TOMÉ AND PRINCIPE	1990		Ind.
SEYCHELLES	1993		Ind.
SLOVAK REPUBLIC	1990		
SLOVENIA	1989		
SOLOMON ISLANDS		1966	Ind.
SOUTH AFRICA	1997	1995	1991
SPAIN	1995	1978	1975
SWEDEN	1972	1921	1910
SWITZERLAND	1992	1942	1944
TUVALU			Ind.
UNITED KINGDOM	1998	1973	1964
URUGUAY	1907		
VANUATU			Ind.
VATICAN CITY STATE	1969		
VENEZUELA	1863		

Source: *The Death Penalty: List of Abolitionist and Retentionist Countries*, 1999, © Amnesty International Publications, 1 Easton Street, London WC1X 0DJ, United Kingdom, www.amnesty.org

China

Amnesty International has reported a massive rise in death sentences in China, resulting from a nationwide anti-crime campaign, which has involved speedier and more stringent punishment. AI claims that "several provinces began their campaigns by retrying and sentencing to death offenders previously sentenced to fixed terms of imprisonment." Moreover, Chinese officials have allegedly been very inconsistent in determining which crimes merited the death penalty.

In October 1999, the Chinese government passed a law allowing the imposition of the death sentence on leaders of the Falun Gong movement charged with endangering national security and murder. The government claimed the "cult" movement has caused the death of over a thousand followers by dissuading them from seeking medical help.

Japan

Amnesty International notes that "executions in Japan ... are carried out without the knowledge of families and appear to be inflicted in an arbitrary fashion." The Japanese government does not announce any pending execution, confirm that one has occurred, or notify families of death row inmates about the impending execution. Even the inmate scheduled to be put to death would only learn of his or her fate on the morning of the execution. Japan is also known for its drawn-out process of appeals. A case that drew worldwide attention involved a prisoner who, in 1997, after having been on death row for 30 years, was executed in secrecy. The inmate had committed multiple murders as a minor of age 19 under Japanese law but was convicted as an adult.

DE FACTO ABOLITIONISTS

Twenty-three countries are considered *de facto* abolitionists (Table 9.2). They have death penalty laws but have not carried out any executions for the past 10 years or more. These countries have abolished capital punishment in practice (*de facto*), although they have not done so legally (*de jure*). Some of these nations have not executed anyone for the past 30 years or more. Others have made an international commitment not to impose the death sentence.

ABOLITIONIST COUNTRIES

In 1863, Venezuela became the first nation to outlaw the death penalty. Since that time, many countries have abolished capital punishment. However, several countries, such as Argentina, Brazil, and Spain, restored it after previously rejecting it. Argentina revoked the death penalty in 1921 and then again in 1972, reinstating it in 1976 after a military takeover. Then, in 1984, it abolished capital punishment again. Brazil abolished the death penalty in 1882, restored it in 1969, and revoked it again in 1979.

Similarly, Spain repealed the death penalty in 1932, restored it for certain crimes in 1934, totally restored it in 1938, and then abolished it again in 1978. The switching back and forth between the abolition and the reimposition of capital punishment often reflects these countries' shift between democracy and dictatorship.

As of December 18, 1999, 70 countries had abolished the death penalty for all crimes (Table 9.3). Many countries have stopped imposing capital punishment since 1976, when the United States reinstated it after a nine-year moratorium. In 1996, Belgium, the last of the western European democracies to have the death sentence, abolished it for all crimes. In reality, Belgium has not executed any prisoner since 1950. Hong Kong went back under Chinese jurisdiction in July 1997. Having abolished capital punishment in 1993, the former British colony remains abolitionist. In 1999, East Timor became an abolitionist nation for all crimes. (See Table 9.4 for a list of the countries that have abolished the death penalty since 1976.)

Abolitionist Countries
for Ordinary Crimes Only

Thirteen countries do not have the death penalty for "ordinary" crimes committed during peacetime (Table 9.5). Over the past decade, five countries — Nepal (1990), South Africa (1995), Bolivia (1997), Bosnia-Herzegovina (1997), and Latvia (1999) — eliminated the death penalty for ordinary crimes. In 1997, Nepal and South Africa abolished the death penalty for all crimes (Table 9.3).

Capital Punishment Is Seldom Reintroduced

Amnesty International notes that once a country abolishes capital punishment, it seldom brings it back. Between 1985 and 1999, 35 countries ei-

TABLE 9.4

COUNTRIES WHICH HAVE ABOLISHED THE DEATH PENALTY SINCE 1976

1976: PORTUGAL abolished the death penalty for all crimes. CANADA abolished the death penalty for ordinary crimes.

1978: DENMARK abolished the death penalty for all crimes. SPAIN abolished the death penalty for ordinary crimes.

1979: LUXEMBOURG, NICARAGUA and NORWAY abolished the death penalty for all crimes. BRAZIL, FIJI and PERU abolished the death penalty for ordinary crimes.

1981: FRANCE and CAPE VERDE abolished the death penalty for all crimes.

1982: The NETHERLANDS abolished the death penalty for all crimes.

1983: CYPRUS and EL SALVADOR abolished the death penalty for ordinary crimes.

1984: ARGENTINA abolished the death penalty for ordinary crimes.

1985: AUSTRALIA abolished the death penalty for all crimes.

1987: HAITI, LIECHTENSTEIN and the GERMAN DEMOCRATIC REPUBLIC (1) abolished the death penalty for all crimes.

1989: CAMBODIA, NEW ZEALAND, ROMANIA and SLOVENIA (2) abolished the death penalty for all crimes.

1990: ANDORRA, CROATIA (2), the CZECH AND SLOVAK FEDERAL REPUBLIC (3), HUNGARY, IRELAND, MOZAMBIQUE, NAMIBIA and SÃO TOMÉ AND PRINCIPE abolished the death penalty for all crimes NEPAL abolished the death penalty for ordinary crimes.

1992: ANGOLA, PARAGUAY and SWITZERLAND abolished the death penalty for all crimes.

1993: GREECE, GUINEA-BISSAU, HONG KONG (4) and SEYCHELLES abolished the death penalty for all crimes.

1994: ITALY abolished the death penalty for all crimes.

1995: MAURITIUS, MOLDOVA and SPAIN abolished the death penalty for all crimes. SOUTH AFRICA abolished the death penalty for ordinary crimes.

1996: BELGIUM abolished the death penalty for all crimes.

1997: GEORGIA, NEPAL, POLAND and SOUTH AFRICA abolished the death penalty for all crimes. BOLIVIA and BOSNIA-HERZEGOVINA abolished the death penalty for ordinary crimes.

1998: AZERBAIJAN, BULGARIA, CANADA, ESTONIA, LITHUANIA and the UNITED KINGDOM abolished the death penalty for all crimes.

1999: EAST TIMOR abolished the death penalty for all crimes. LATVIA (5) abolished the death penalty for ordinary crimes only.

Notes:

1. In 1990 the German Democratic Republic became unified with the Federal Republic of Germany, where the death penalty had been abolished in 1949.

2. Slovenia and Croatia abolished the death penalty while they were still republics of the Socialist Federal Republic of Yugoslavia. The two republics became independent in 1991.

3. In 1993 the Czech and Slovak Federal Republic divided into two states, the Czech Republic and Slovakia.

4. In 1997 Hong Kong was returned to Chinese rule as a special administrative region of China. Amnesty International understands that Hong Kong will remain abolitionist.

5. In 1999 the Latvian parliament voted to ratify Protocol No. 6 to the European Convention on Human Rights, abolishing the death penalty for peacetime offences.

Source: *The Death Penalty: List of Abolitionist and Retentionist Countries*, 1999, © Amnesty International Publications, 1 Easton Street, London WC1X 0DJ, United Kingdom, www.amnesty.org

TABLE 9.5

ABOLITIONIST FOR ORDINARY CRIMES ONLY

Abbreviations: **Date (AO)** = date of abolition for ordinary crimes; **Date (last ex.)** = date of last execution; **K** = date of last known execution; **Ind.** = no executions since independence

Country	Date (AO)	Date (last ex.)
ARGENTINA	1984	
BOLIVIA	1997	1974
BOSNIA-HERZEGOVINA	1997	
BRAZIL	1979	1855
COOK ISLANDS		
CYPRUS	1983	1962
EL SALVADOR	1983	1973 K
FIJI	1979	1964
ISRAEL	1954	1962
LATVIA	1999	1996
MALTA	1971	1943
MEXICO		1937
PERU	1979	1979

Source: *The Death Penalty: List of Abolitionist and Retentionist Countries*, 1999, © Amnesty International Publications, 1 Easton Street, London WC1X 0DJ, United Kingdom, www.amnesty.org

ther enacted laws abolishing the death penalty or, having revoked it for ordinary crimes, eventually outlawed it for all crimes. In 1994, the Philippines reintroduced the death penalty. In February 1999, the first execution since 1976 took place, followed by four others. Pending review of death penalty cases, President Joseph Estrada suspended all executions effective August 1999.

DEATH PENALTY AGAINST MINORS

According to Amnesty International, over the last 10 years, the execution of prisoners who were under age 18 at the time of the commission of their crimes has continued in eight countries — Bangladesh, Iran, Iraq, Nigeria, Pakistan, Saudi Arabia, the United States, and Yemen. The major-ity of executions have occurred in the United States (see Chapter V).

AI claims that these countries are violating international human rights agreements. The International Covenant on Civil and Political Rights, the United Nations Convention on the Rights of the Child, and the American Convention on Human Rights all ban the imposition of the death sentence on persons who were less than 18 years old at the time of the crime. The UN Convention on the Rights of the Child further prohibits the sentence of life without the possibility of parole for those less than 18 years old. Today, virtually all countries in the world either have statutes prohibiting the execution of minors or are believed to be abiding by the provisions of one or another of the above treaties.

CHAPTER X

THE DEBATE — CAPITAL PUNISHMENT SHOULD BE MAINTAINED

STATEMENT OF FLORIDA GOVERNOR JEB BUSH REGARDING U.S. SUPREME COURT'S DISMISSAL OF *BRYAN V. MOORE* (NO. 99-6723), JANUARY 24, 2000

The U.S. Supreme Court today dismissed the case, *Bryan v. Moore* (No. 99-6723; see Chapter V), which would have reviewed the constitutionality of Florida's electric chair.

Earlier this month, the Florida Legislature passed, and I signed, a precedent-setting action providing two alternative methods of execution, lethal injection or the electric chair. As a result, the U.S. Supreme Court has determined this challenge to Florida's electric chair case should be dismissed.

As I have said before, I believe that Florida's electric chair is constitutional and is an appropriate means of punishment for the heinous crimes where the death penalty is imposed. Now that the state of Florida provides two appropriate methods of execution, if an inmate chooses the electric chair, all legal challenges claiming cruel and unusual punishment are moot.

I am confident that we can finally put an end to the unnecessary and endless delays long associated with death penalty cases in Florida. It is time to bring justice to the families of victims who have suffered and died at the hands of the most heinous criminals.

LETTER WRITTEN BY STATE SENATOR RON KLEIN (D-FL) TO GOVERNOR JEB BUSH TO CONSIDER LETHAL INJECTION AS THE METHOD OF EXECUTION, JULY 12, 1999

For those of us who are strong proponents of capital punishment, once due process has been met, a quick and efficient means of execution is an absolute requirement in order to sufficiently create the deterrent which is intended. Every time the constitutionality of the electric chair is challenged, we jeopardize the swift implementation of justice, undermine the impact and deterrence value of a death sentence, and prolong the pain and suffering of victims' families. We should, once and for all, adopt lethal injection as the means of execution in Florida for all future death warrants.

Each time we execute an inmate in Florida by electrocution, we risk the potential of another mishap that will be the catalyst for additional stays and delays. The method of execution should not take priority over the most efficient, constitutional means of carrying out a death sentence. I have said many times before that "dead is dead."

Lethal injection is being successfully administered as the sole method of execution in 16 states and as a choice in 16 others. In Texas, for example, 128 inmates (more than any other state in the nation) were executed by lethal injection without incident between 1977 and 1997. Over 77 percent of executions nationwide are now carried out by lethal injection because it has met constitutional muster over and over again.

It is time for Florida to take the issue of the electric chair, which is forcing delays, appeals and stays, out of the equation. By providing timely and efficient justice, we can begin to send a strong message to criminals and accomplish the goal with which the public has charged us.

I look forward to your support and leadership on this issue during the upcoming legislative session.

STATEMENT OF HENRY J. HYDE (R-IL), CHAIRMAN, HOUSE OF REPRESENTATIVES JUDICIARY COMMITTEE, DECEMBER 10, 1997

With regard to the issue of capital punishment, it is my view that the death penalty, if imposed fairly and without undue delay, can serve a deterrent purpose in our criminal justice system. There are some cases of murder that are so heinous and brutal that society must impose its ultimate penalty. These cases would include terrorism, treason, hijacking resulting in the death of a hostage, or the killing of a police [officer] or prison guard acting in the line of duty. If, under careful deliberation, it is determined that such a crime has occurred and the defendant in the crime has been proven guilty beyond a reasonable doubt, then I would support the imposition of capital punishment.

Society has a right to impose whatever punishment it collectively determines befits the violation of its laws. Denying society the ability to impose the death penalty on those convicted of murder devalues the lives of its citizens.

STATEMENT OF SENATOR DON NICKLES (R-OK) AFTER THE OKLAHOMA CITY BOMBER, TIMOTHY MCVEIGH, WAS SENTENCED TO DEATH, JUNE 13, 1997

Oklahomans everywhere breathed a deep sigh of relief when Denver jurors found Timothy McVeigh guilty of the Oklahoma City bombing recently.

It is no longer speculation that McVeigh is guilty of the most horrific case of domestic terrorism in our nation's history. His murderous and carefully plotted attack against America killed 169 people, including 19 children. We will always remember their faces, treasure their lives, and honor their dreams and hopes. And we will help bear the physical and emotional burdens of more than 460 others who were scarred and injured in the blast.

Now, Oklahoma turns its attention toward making sure McVeigh's sentence is carried out fully and taking another step toward putting the tragedy behind us....

I am ... pleased by the legislative changes passed by Congress in the wake of the Oklahoma City bombing. The Oklahoma congressional delegation was unified in our work to provide trial coverage on closed-circuit television; give survivors and victims' family members the ability to both view a trial and testify during the sentencing phase; and strengthen penalties for the use of explosive devices and killing federal law officers. Importantly, Congress also curbed the nearly limitless stream of appeals by death row inmates.

STATEMENT OF REPRESENTATIVE ROBERT K. DORNAN (R-CA), DECEMBER 4, 1995

As a U.S. congressman, one of my primary concerns is the rule of law. Over the last 30 years, our nation has experienced a crippling decline in effective law enforcement resulting from the erosion of the concept of swift and sure punishment for law breakers. This has resulted from multiple causes, including a politicized judiciary, which all too often has been more sympathetic to the criminal than the victim, and as well, to a general judicial philosophy which has become more concerned with questions of procedure than the search for truth....

As a conservative, I believe there are certain crimes for which the death penalty is justified. Some individuals commit crimes so reprehensible that they forfeit their right to live in society. And some commit crimes so heinous that they do not deserve to be supported for life by the society they injured. These are the people who should be sentenced to death. The death penalty should remain our most severe punishment and should be used only in extraordinary cases. But as has always been the standard in our justice system, the punishment should fit the crime.

STATEMENT OF REPRESENTATIVE SAM JOHNSON (R-TX), NOVEMBER 8, 1995

Regarding capital punishment, I continue to believe that the best way to prevent crime is to target repeat offenders. Criminals must understand the consequences of their actions. We should make prisoners serve out their entire sentences and enforce stiffer penalties, such as capital punishment against felons convicted of heinous crimes, such as rape, murder, and drug-related deaths. I am aware of the need for individual responsibility in determining the death penalty's applicability, and we must always be diligent not to punish the innocent. However, in spite of these risks, I believe that capital punishment is a morally justifiable, necessary, and effective punishment.

Thirty-six states currently administer capital punishment. Texas alone has executed 99 criminals in the past seven years. The people of Texas have made it known that violent crime will not be tolerated.

STATEMENT OF SENATOR JESSE HELMS (R-SC), NOVEMBER 6, 1995

Although I wish that the death penalty was never necessary, I do believe that it should be available to our courts to punish those responsible for especially violent crimes. I believe that the death penalty protects society from further harm by the offender. I also think that it is useful in deterring others from committing similar crimes.

American society will be increasingly plagued by violent crime without the use of the death penalty. In order to combat crime, we must give our police officers and judges the support and encouragement necessary to get tough with criminals. The death penalty is one step in the *right* direction.

EXCERPTS FROM JUSTICE ANTONIN SCALIA'S CONCURRING OPINION IN THE SUPREME COURT DECISION *CALLINS V. JAMES* (510 U.S. 1141, 1994), DENYING REVIEW OF THE DEATH PENALTY CASE (IN RESPONSE TO JUSTICE BLACKMUN'S DISSENT; SEE CHAPTER XI)

The Fifth Amendment provides that "[n]o persons shall be held to answer for a capital crime, unless on a presentment or indictment of a Grand Jury ... nor be deprived of life ... without due process of law." This clearly permits the death penalty to be imposed and establishes beyond doubt that the death penalty is not one of the "cruel and unusual punishments" prohibited by the Eighth Amendment.

Convictions in opposition to the death penalty are often passionate and deeply held. That would be no excuse for reading them into a Constitution that does not contain them, even if they represented the convictions of a majority of Americans. Much less is there any excuse for using that course to thrust a minority's views upon the people. Justice Blackmun ... describ[es] with poignancy the death of a convicted murderer by lethal injection. He chooses ... one of the less brutal of the murders — the murder of a man ripped by a bullet suddenly and unexpectedly, with no opportunity to prepare himself and his affairs, and left to bleed to death on the floor of a tavern. The death-by-injection, which Justice Blackmun describes, looks pretty desirable next to that. It looks even better next to some of the other cases currently before us, which Justice Blackmun did not select as the vehicle for his announcement that the death penalty is always unconstitutional — for example, the case of the 11-year-old girl raped by four men and then killed.... How enviable a quiet death by lethal injection compared with that! If the people conclude ... that ... brutal deaths may be deterred by capital punishment, indeed, if they merely conclude that justice requires such brutal deaths to be avenged by capital punishment, the creation of false, untextual, and unhistorical contradictions within the "Court's Eighth Amendment jurisprudence" should not prevent them.

STATEMENT OF PAUL G. CASSELL, ASSOCIATE PROFESSOR OF LAW, UNIVERSITY OF UTAH, SALT LAKE CITY, BEFORE THE SENATE JUDICIARY COMMITTEE, APRIL 1, 1993

The paucity (smallness of number) of examples of innocent defendants who have been executed provides compelling evidence that the risk of mistaken execution is virtually non-existent. If opponents of the death penalty are able to produce no better examples of mistaken executions [in the testimony], then the overwhelming majority of Americans who support capital punishment can rest assured that the criminal justice system is doing an admirable, if not indeed perfect, job of preventing the execution of innocent defendants....

Capital sentences, when carried out, save innocent lives by permanently incapacitating murderers. Some persons who commit capital homicide will slay other innocent persons if given the opportunity to do so. The death penalty is the most effective means of preventing such killers from repeating their crimes. The next most serious penalty, life imprisonment without possibility of parole, prevents murderers from committing some crimes but does not prevent them from murdering in prison.

At least five federal prison officers have been killed since December 1982, and the inmates in at least three of the incidents were already serving life sentences for murder....

While the innocent lives saved through the incapacitative effect of capital punishment are important, the penalty also saves far more innocent lives through its general deterrent effect....

Logic supports the conclusion that the death penalty is the most effective deterrent for some kinds of murders — those that require reflection and forethought by persons of reasonable intelligence and unimpaired mental facilities. Many capital offenses are quintessential (the most typical) contemplative offenses. Murder for hire, treason, and terrorist bombings all require extensive planning. It stands to reason that capital punishment deters such persons more than the next most serious penalty, life imprisonment without parole.

Anecdotal evidence in support of the deterrent value of capital sentences comes from examples of persons who have been deterred from murdering, or risking a murder, because of the death penalty. For instance, Justice McComb of the California Supreme Court collected from the files of the Los Angeles Police Department 14 examples within a four-year period of defendants who, in explaining their refusal to take a life or carry a weapon, pointed to the presence of the death penalty....

Statistical studies support the proposition that capital sentences, like other criminal sanctions, have a deterrent effect. To be sure, some statistical surveys, often conducted by opponents of the death penalty, have found no such effect....

One of the most recent substantial econometric studies (applying statistical methods to economics to study problems) was performed by Professor Stephen K. Layson of the University of North Carolina at Greensboro, who analyzed data for the United States from 1936 to 1977. Layson concluded that increases in the probability of execution reduced the homicide rate. Specifically, Layson found that, on average, each execution deterred approximately 18 murders....

Through the imposition of just punishment, civilized society expresses its outrage and sense of revulsion toward those who, by contravening (violating) its laws, have not only inflicted injury upon discrete (separate and distinct) individuals, but also weakened the bonds that hold communities together. Certain crimes constitute such outrageous violation of human and moral values that they demand retribution. It was to control the natural human impulse to seek revenge and, more broadly, to give expression to deeply held views that some conduct deserves punishment, that criminal laws, administered by the state, were established. The rule of law does not eliminate feelings of outrage but does provide controlled channels for expressing such feelings. People can rely on society to sanction criminal conduct and to carry out deserved punishments....

The death penalty's retributive function thus vindicates the fundamental moral principle that a criminal should receive his or her just desserts. Through the provision of just punishment, capital punishment affirms the sanctity of human life and thereby protects it.

... [T]he system imposes a vast array of due process protections to assure that no innocent person is convicted of a crime.

STATEMENT OF MIRIAM SHEHANE, STATE PRESIDENT, VICTIMS OF CRIME AND LENIENCY, MONTGOMERY, ALABAMA, BEFORE THE SENATE JUDICIARY COMMITTEE, APRIL 1, 1993

My daughter, Quenette, was brutally murdered in 1976....

Time will not permit nor will I burden you with the gory details of how one of the defendants described her hours of torture and final death, but the memory is imprinted in my mind permanently. The three men who killed her were arrested and brought to trial — literally seven trials over a period of six years.... The frustrations the families go through when they think justice will soon prevail, only to receive jolt after jolt as they learn the case is going back for trial due to technicalities, [are] enough to cause fatal health problems.

... As you know, 36 states have determined that the death penalty is the most appropriate punishment for certain brutal and vicious murders. As the parent of a murder victim, I feel this punishment is not only fair, it is essential. What is not fair is when this punishment is prolonged by extensive appeals, stays, and postponements. We vic-

tims need a closure to our grief. I did not rejoice when Wallace Norrell was executed July 13, 1990, for murdering Quenette, but I certainly felt relief. I could not have a sense of completion and finally put my dear Quenette to rest if I didn't have to [sic] worry about two others being released at some point....

I can assure you that the system, as it now operates, gives far more consideration to death row inmates than it affords the victims and their families. What are the safeguards for the victim when a murderer is tried, acquitted by a jury, but can never be retried no matter how much evidence is produced in the future? Are the scales of justice earnestly balanced when a convicted murderer is not executed for 13 1/2 years? Lest we forget, in addition to the extensive appeals of the courts, every state with a capital punishment statute has a procedure for executive clemency....

STATEMENT OF BRUCE FEIN, PRIVATE ATTORNEY SPECIALIZING IN CONSTITUTIONAL AND COMMUNICATIONS LAWS, BEFORE THE HOUSE JUDICIARY COMMITTEE, MAY 23, 1990

... [A]lthough the death penalty certainly is not the answer to the worrisome ... levels of crime today, it is an important tool, I think, in creating a right kind of moral climate that suggests there are certain standards of behavior that must be accepted in order to avoid degeneration of society, anarchy, and a level of bestiality....

We must recognize that death laws have tongues. They speak to a moral universe that places some kind of conduct simply beyond the level of decent mankind....

It seems to me as well that certainly when you speak of the need for a death penalty for [killing] prison wardens, that would not threaten somebody who is already in prison under a life term with no possibility of parole, and who has very little incentive to do anything to control his conduct, to try to escape, to kill to escape because there isn't any further punishment that is available if death is not an option.

I think we owe a certain decency toward our prison wardens who undertake very dangerous positions to have that death penalty option there.

STATEMENT OF JOHN C. SCULLY, COUNSEL, WASHINGTON LEGAL FOUNDATION, WASHINGTON, DC, BEFORE THE HOUSE JUDICIARY COMMITTEE, MAY 3, 1990

The overwhelming majority of Americans, Black and White, support the death penalty. The Supreme Court has consistently upheld the constitutionality of the death penalty. The drug-war killings and the other murders that occur daily in our country demonstrate the need for the death penalty. The death penalty is a deterrent to future murders. Finally, some murders are so shocking that it is evident that there is no other punishment that fits the crime.

Yet, the will of the majority of the people is regularly frustrated by the opponents of the death penalty who repeatedly devise new and often bizarre forms of lethal attacks upon the death penalty. The rejection by the U.S. Supreme Court of the statistical disparity-death-by-racial-quota theory has led the anti-death penalty advocates to seek a legislative vehicle to attack the death penalty....

WLF [Washington Legal Foundation] strongly opposes racial discrimination in the justice system. Individuals sentenced to death should and do have the right and opportunity to challenge any act of racial discrimination in the justice system.

... The BJS [Bureau of Justice Statistics] report showed that for every 1,000 Whites arrested on homicide charges, approximately 16 were given a death sentence, while fewer than 12 Blacks were sent to death row for every 1,000 Blacks arrested for homicide. This means that White murderers are 36 percent more likely to be sentenced to death than their Black counterparts.

Does that mean that White murderers are the victims of racial discrimination? Of course not. There are numerous individual circumstances that comprise each murder case; those circumstances make it impossible to use statistics to prove discrimination in a manner similar to that utilized in employment discrimination cases.

... Studies, unable to show racial discrimination against Blacks by examining the race of the defendant, also examined the race of the victim. The *Baldus Study* concluded that for some types of murders, if the victim of the crime was White, then the murderer was more likely to receive a death sentence than if the victim was Black.

The race-of-the-victim theory, if accepted, means that even a White murderer can level charges of racism at a jury that sent him to death row for killing a White person....

The Katz study showed that the Black defendant/White victim cases are the most aggravated of the four defendant-victim racial combinations. The interracial nature of this kind of homicide minimized the possibility that the killing arose due to a family dispute or fight between friends, neighbors, or relatives.

The Black defendant/Black victim homicides occurred most frequently and were characterized by poor defendants who kill family members, friends, or other acquaintances during a fight or argument. Those types of murders generally have the most mitigating circumstances.

The White defendant/White victim homicides reflected a mix between killings precipitated by a dispute similar to those precipitating Black-on-Black homicides, but with a substantial percent (about one-third) of the killings comparable to the Black-on-White homicides.

Only 27 of the 1,082 cases were characterized as White defendant/Black victim homicides. The relatively small number of such homicides made them difficult for Katz to classify.

STATEMENT OF JAMES C. ANDERS, SO-LICITOR, FIFTH JUDICIAL CIRCUIT OF SOUTH CAROLINA, BEFORE THE SENATE JUDICIARY COMMITTEE, SEPTEMBER 19, 1989

I believe that in certain cases, the death penalty can be shown to be the only rational and realistic punishment for an unspeakable crime.... Obviously, the most basic right a citizen has is the right to be secure in his person, the right to be safe from physical or economic harm from another. Laws to protect citizens and advance the harmony of society are founded upon these principles. To enforce these laws, created in the best interest of society as a whole, there has to be a deterrent for a breach of the law. Therefore, deterrence is the first aim of a system of punishment.

Deterrence is only one side of the punishment coin, however. An equally fundamental reason to punish lies in society's compelling desire to see justice done. Punishment expresses the emotions of the society wronged, the anger and outrage felt, and it solidifies and reinforces the goals, values, and norms of acceptable behavior in the society....

The deterrent effect of the death penalty is the favorite criticism of the opponents of capital punishment. The social scientists' studies have been mixed at best, and there is no authoritative consensus on whether or not the death penalty deters anyone from committing a crime. Threats of punishment cannot and are not meant to deter everybody all of the time. They are meant to deter most people most of the time. Therefore, the death penalty can only be a deterrent if it is meted out with a reasonable degree of consistency. The deterrence effect lies in the knowledge of the citizenry that it will more likely than not be carried out if the named crime is committed.

Even if one is not fully convinced of the deterrent effect of the death penalty, he or she would surely choose the certainty of the convicted criminal's death by execution over the possibility of the deaths of new victims.

Death penalty opponents argue that if life is sacred, then the murderer's life, too, is sacred ... and for the state to punish him by execution is barbaric and causes the state to bend to the murderer's level. The only similarity between the unjustified taking of an innocent life and the carrying out of a convicted murderer's execution is the end result — death. The death penalty is a legal sentence, enacted by the legislatures of various states, which presumably reflect their constituents' desires. It is a penalty that can finally be carried out only after a trial where the defendant is afforded all of his constitutional rights....

Death penalty opponents are also troubled by the studies that purport to show that the death penalty is applied capriciously (unpredictably), that it discriminates racially and economically.... Assuming that premise for the sake of argument, is that a rational reason to abolish the death penalty? Is the fact that some guilty persons escape punishment sufficient to let all guilty persons escape it?

... If the death penalty can deter one murder of an innocent life or if it can make a statement to the community about what will and will not be tolerated, then it is justified.

Opponents of the death penalty advocate the life sentence in prison as a viable alternative to execution.... Early release programs, furloughs, and escape combine to place a shockingly high number of convicted murderers back on the streets in record time.

The life without parole sentence is no solution either. First, the possibility of escape cannot be completely eliminated, even in the most secure of institutions.... Second, the life without parole sentence places a tremendous burden on prison administrators. Faced with controlling inmates who have already received the worst punishment society can mete out, they can only throw their hands up in frustration. Lastly, the true lifer is not only capable of continuing to murder, but may actually be more likely to do so. Every prison in the country has its own stories of the lifer who killed another inmate over a cigarette or a piece of chicken.

STATEMENT OF ROBERT B. KLIESMET, PRESIDENT, INTERNATIONAL UNION OF POLICE ASSOCIATIONS, BEFORE THE SENATE JUDICIARY COMMITTEE, SEPTEMBER 19, 1989

Street cops, in their pragmatic view, believe, as does 86 percent of the public, that the death penalty is a viable deterrent for persons convicted of certain crimes. A search of the literature shows there are a number of studies and articles that show a direct deterrent effect by imposing and carrying out the death penalty. One study goes as far as to point out that for each execution for a homicide, up to 15 lives can be saved through the deterrent effect. The safety of society, which is the real goal of the criminal justice system, is being compromised by saving the life of a convicted offender. This compromise is a needless sacrifice of a blameless victim's life.

STATEMENT OF NEWT GINGRICH (R-GA), JANUARY 31, 1988

... [The state] should use the death penalty for such serious crimes as murder and treason. Criminals might think twice before committing such acts if they knew that the consequences of their actions could result in the death penalty. People must be held accountable for the crimes they commit. I don't believe we can just slap someone on the hand and hope [he or she] never misbehave[s] again.

Right now, there are over a thousand prisoners on death row. Many of them have been there since the early 1970s because our current criminal justice system encourages them to seek endless appeals in order to delay their sentence of death.

I believe this is wrong. That's why I'm working on legislation to establish a unified appeals process that would place a two-year time limit on appeals to federal courts. This would prevent persons convicted of crimes from deliberately dragging out their appeals simply to delay the death sentence.

STATEMENT OF SENATOR JOHN P. EAST (R-NC), JANUARY 16, 1986

With the tougher attitude towards crime that we have taken in the past five years, the murder rate has gone down, but day after day we still read newspaper accounts of murders, many of which are carried out with chilling cruelty and detachment. The American people deserve continued protection from this wave of killing, protection often denied them by a system that often still gives lenient penalties to the most vicious criminals.

Death is the only suitable penalty for reprehensible crimes, such as premeditated murder. Murder does not simply differ in magnitude from extortion or theft. It differs in kind as well, and its punishment also should differ in kind. Murderers have not simply injured their victims, but they have weakened the most important bond that holds communities together — respect for life. By imposing the supreme penalty in cases of murder, society expresses its moral outrage at such a crime; it sends a signal that innocent human life is precious; and it declares that such life cannot be violated without a like consequence to the killer. By imposing the death penalty, it also deters other would-be murderers, and it prevents the murderer from killing again.

I am convinced that there needs to be a federal death penalty statute. In particular, we need to be able to impose the death penalty for the assassination of high government officials. We also need to provide for capital punishment in cases where convicted killers, already confined in a federal prison and serving life sentences, commit murder again. At present, such people have no incentive not to kill because they are already suffering the severest penalty that federal law has to offer. As a result, the number of gruesome murders at federal correctional institutions is on the rise.

TESTIMONY OF ERNEST VAN DEN HAAG, ADJUNCT PROFESSOR OF SOCIAL PHILOSOPHY, NEW YORK UNIVERSITY, BEFORE THE SUBCOMMITTEE ON CRIMI-

NAL LAW AND PROCEDURES OF THE SENATE JUDICIARY COMMITTEE, MARCH 15, 1972

It is suggested that the death penalty discriminates against the poor and the Black.... If true, ... the suggestion would be nonetheless wholly irrelevant. It concerns the unfair way in which the penalty is distributed, not the fairness or unfairness of the penalty.

Any penalty ... could be unfairly or unjustly applied. The vice is not in the penalty, but in the process by which it is inflicted. It is unfair to inflict unequal penalties on equally guilty parties, or on any innocent parties, regardless of what the penalty is.... You should try to correct the judicial processes by which, it is alleged, the penalties are unfairly inflicted....

All penalties — including fines, prison sentences, and the death penalty — are deterrent roughly in proportion to their severity.... Were that not the case, we would certainly not have varied penalties, but might impose a uniform penalty of $5 for any crime whatsoever. We impose penalties roughly differentiated because we feel that crimes of different gravity deserve different punishment.

On the basis of the statistics available, no logical conclusion one way or the other can be reached. It cannot be proven that the death penalty is additionally deterrent; it cannot be proven either that it is not....

No penalty can deter the irrational, perhaps. But penalties do influence those who are rational enough to be influenced. In this respect the data suggest the death penalty has been very effective, precisely because very few murders are committed by rational persons.

CHAPTER XI

THE DEBATE — CAPITAL PUNISHMENT SHOULD BE ABOLISHED

A JOINT STATEMENT, *TO END THE DEATH PENALTY*, BY THE NATIONAL JEWISH/CATHOLIC CONSULTATION (CO-SPONSORED BY THE NATIONAL COUNCIL OF SYNAGOGUES AND THE BISHOPS' COMMITTEE FOR ECUMENICAL AND INTERRELIGIOUS AFFAIRS OF THE NATIONAL CONFERENCE OF CATHOLIC BISHOPS), DECEMBER 3, 1999

"A Sanhedrin (Jewish court of law) that puts one person to death once in seven years is called destructive. Rabbi Eliezer ben Azariah says: Or even once in seventy years. Rabbi Tarfon and Rabbi Akiba say: Had we been the Sanhedrin, none would ever have been put to death." *Mishnah Makkot, 1:10 (2nd Century, C.E.)*

"A sign of hope is the increasing recognition that the dignity of human life must never be taken away, even in the case of someone who has done great evil. Modern society has the means of protecting itself, without definitively denying criminals the chance to reform. I renew the appeal for a consensus to end the death penalty, which is both cruel and unnecessary." *Pope John Paul II, January 27, 1999, St. Louis, Missouri*

Almost two millennia separate these two statements, which together embody the collective wisdom and moral insights of our two ancient religious traditions, Rabbinic Judaism and Roman Catholicism, on a burning issue of our time, capital punishment. At our meeting of March 23, 1999, we religious leaders, Catholic and Jewish, probed and shared our own traditions with each other. (The National Jewish/Catholic Consultation has been meeting twice a year since 1987.) The result was a remarkable confluence of witness on how best in our time to interpret the eternal word of God.

Both traditions begin with an affirmation of the sanctity of human life. Both, as the above statements imply, acknowledge the theoretical possibility of a justifiable death penalty, since the Scriptures mandate it for certain offenses. Yet both have, over the centuries, narrowed those grounds until, today, we would say together that it is time to cease the practice altogether. To achieve this consensus (majority opinion), we analyzed the statements of our respective bodies going back to the late 1970s and we agree that in them we found a growing conviction that the arguments offered in defense of the death penalty are less than persuasive in the face of the overwhelming mandate in both Jewish and Catholic traditions to respect the sanctity of human life.

Some would argue that the death penalty is needed as a means of retributive justice (exacting punishment for offense done) to balance out the crime with the punishment. This reflects a natural concern of society, and especially of victims and their families. Yet we believe that we are called to seek a higher road even while punishing the guilty, for example through long and in some cases life-long incarceration, so that the healing of all can ultimately take place.

Some would argue that the death penalty is needed as a deterrent to crime. Yet the studies that lie behind our statements over the years have yet to reveal any objective evidence to justify this conclusion. Criminals tend to believe they will escape any consequences for their behavior, or simply do not think of consequences at all, so an escalation of consequences is usually irrelevant to their state of mind at the time of the crime.

Some would argue that the death penalty will teach society at large the seriousness of crime. Yet we say that teaching people to respond to violence with violence will, again, only breed more violence.

Some would argue that our system of justice, trial by jury, can ensure that capital punishment will be meted out equitably (fairly) to various groups in society and that the innocent will never be convicted. This is the least persuasive argument of all. Statistics, however weighted, indicate that errors are made in judgment and convictions. Recent scientific advances, such as DNA testing, may reveal that persons on death row, despite seemingly "overwhelming" circumstantial evidence, may in fact be innocent of the charges against them. Likewise, suspiciously high percentages of those on death row are poor or people of color. Our legal system is a very good one, but it is a human institution. Even a small percentage of irreversible errors is increasingly seen as intolerable. God alone is the author of life.

The strongest argument of all is the deep pain and grief of the families of victims and their quite natural desire to see punishment meted out to those who have plunged them into such agony. Yet it is the clear teaching of our traditions that this pain and suffering cannot be healed simply through the retribution of capital punishment or by vengeance. It is a difficult and long process of healing, which comes about through personal growth and God's grace. We agree that much more must be done by the religious community and by society at large to solace and care for the grieving families of the victims of violent crime.

… We affirm that we came to these conclusions because of our shared understanding of the sanctity of human life. We have committed ourselves to work together, and each within our own communities, toward ending the death penalty.

STATEMENT OF SENATOR RUSSELL FEINGOLD (D-WI), ON INTRODUCING THE FEDERAL DEATH PENALTY ABOLITION ACT OF 1999 (S. 1917) BEFORE THE SENATE, NOVEMBER 10, 1999

… I rise today to introduce the Federal Death Penalty Abolition Act of 1999. This bill will abolish the death penalty at the federal level. It will put an immediate halt to executions and forbid the imposition of the death penalty as a sentence for violations of federal law.

… [A] culture of violence has … infected our nation. As schoolhouse killings have shown, our children now can be reached by that culture of violence. And they aren't just casual observers; some of them are active participants, and many have been victims.

But, … I'm not so sure that we in government don't contribute to this casual attitude we sometimes see toward killing and death. With each new death penalty statute enacted and each execution carried out, our executive, judicial, and legislative branches, at both the state and federal level, add to a culture of violence and killing. With each person executed, we're teaching our children that the way to settle scores is through violence, even to the point of taking a human life.

… Those who favor the death penalty should be pressed to explain why fallible human beings should presume to use the power of the state to extinguish the life of a fellow human being on our collective behalf. Those who oppose the death penalty should demand that explanation adamantly, and at every turn. But only a zealous few try.

… Following the logic of death penalty supporters who believe it's a deterrent, you would think that our European allies, who don't use the death penalty, would have a higher murder rate than the United States. Yet, they don't and it's not even close. In fact, the murder rate in the United States is six times higher than the murder rate in Britain, seven times higher than in France, five times higher than in Australia, and five times higher than in Sweden.

But we don't even need to look across the Atlantic to see that capital punishment has no deterrent effect on crime. Let's compare Wisconsin and Texas.... Wisconsin has been death penalty-free for nearly 150 years. In contrast, Texas is the most prodigious (great in extent) user of the death penalty, having executed 192 people since 1976.... During the period 1995 to 1998, Texas has had a murder rate that is nearly double the murder rate in Wisconsin....

... Some argue that the discovery of the innocence of a death row inmate proves that the system works. This is absurd. How can you say the criminal justice system works when a group of students — not lawyers or investigators but students with no special powers, who were very much outside the system — discover[ed] that a man about to be executed was in fact innocent? That's what happened in Illinois to Ronald Jones. The system doesn't work. It has failed us.

... The Supreme Court has been narrowly focused on procedural technicalities, ignoring the fact that the death penalty is a unique punishment that cannot be undone to correct mistakes. One disturbing decision was issued by the Supreme Court just a few months ago. In *Jones v. United States* [119 S. Ct. 1215, 1999], which involved an inmate on death row in Texas and the interpretation of the 1994 Federal Death Penalty Act, the judge refused to tell the jury that if they deadlocked on the sentence, the law required the judge to impose a sentence of life without possibility of parole. As a result, some jurors were under the grave misunderstanding that lack of unanimity would mean the judge could give a sentence where the defendant might one day go free. The Supreme Court, however, upheld the lower court's imposition of the death penalty....

... Another reason we need to abolish the death penalty is the continuing racism in our criminal justice system.... Of [the] 21 defendants on the federal government's death row, 14 are Black and only five are White. One defendant is Hispanic and another Asian. That means 16 of the 21 people on federal death row are minorities. That's just over 75 percent. And the numbers are worse on the military's death row. Seven of the eight, or 87.5 percent, on military death row are minorities.

... At the end of 1999, at the end of a remarkable century and millennium of progress, I cannot help but believe that our progress has been tarnished with our nation's not only continuing, but increasing use of the death penalty.... We are a nation that prides itself on the fundamental principles of justice, liberty, equality, and due process. We are a nation that scrutinizes the human rights records of other nations. We are one of the first nations to speak out against torture and killings by foreign governments. It is time for us to look in the mirror....

STATEMENT OF SAMUEL JORDAN, DIRECTOR, PROGRAM TO ABOLISH THE DEATH PENALTY, AMNESTY INTERNATIONAL U.S.A., MARCH 4, 1998

The death penalty as imposed in the United States has the power to mislead even the most attentive social observer. Despite its fatal brutality, the death penalty is permitted by the Constitution, honored by custom, and upheld by the courts — as was slavery. Beneath the veneer, the practice of executions is accompanied by a resolute defiance of internationally accepted standards of human rights and fairness.

Repeatedly, studies have shown that capital punishment is imposed arbitrarily with disproportionate weight given to race — of the victim. Although African-Americans account for 50 percent of the homicide victims in the nation, 82 percent of death row offenders have been convicted for the murder of Whites. Poverty as well as race often

102

determines the allocation of the death sentence. Inadequate, inexperienced representation for indigent (poor) defendants characterizes most capital litigation. In addition, imposition of the death penalty often costs as much as three times the expense of lifetime incarceration. The system of executions has also sought to lower the age of offenders against whom it may be applied, thus ensnaring juveniles. And sadly, there are no reliable statistics on the numbers of mentally deficient victims of the executioner.

Many organizations have begun to support the call for a moratorium on the death penalty. They argue that the same conditions persist today, which led the U.S. Supreme Court to order a moratorium on executions in 1972 in the landmark case, *Furman v. Georgia*. The resumption of executions after *Gregg v. Georgia* in 1976 has not been marked by the abatement of racial disparities, arbitrariness, and substandard representation in the judicial process leading to the death sentence. (See Chapter II.)

While the moratorium effort draws attention to the shortcomings of the judicial process, we must not rely upon the courts alone to settle matters of public morality and human rights. The role of the abolitionist in the struggle to rid our nation of the death penalty is not unlike the task that confronted abolitionists in the era of chattel slavery (slaves were treated as personal property) in the United States. The answer will not be found in the law. Laws which permit executions must be changed. They must reflect instead an attempt by our society to respect and enhance the dignity of human life without regard to race, wealth, and prestige.

The first challenge for the modern abolitionist is to topple the death penalty from its pedestal of broad, popular acceptance and to expose it for what it is, a brutal and dehumanizing rationale for legal murder. Next, we must demand that all sectors of the society, especially religious organizations, take command of the moral and humanitarian dimensions of this issue. In the end, to be successful, we must drive a wedge between those who promote capital punishment for selfish reasons, including vote totals and public image, and those who might honestly believe that there is a connection between the death penalty and fairness.

Meeting these challenges will release enormous social energies which can be employed to change the laws. Only then will we join the 101 of the 194 nations of the world which have abandoned the practice of state-sanctioned killing. (At this writing, Azerbaydzhan and the Ukraine had also abolished their death penalty.) We deserve a criminal justice system free of the ritual of human sacrifice.

STATEMENT OF RICHARD C. DIETER, EXECUTIVE DIRECTOR, DEATH PENALTY INFORMATION CENTER, WASHINGTON, DC, DECEMBER 31, 1997

... As the number of executions reached a record high, the discriminatory nature of the death penalty became more apparent. Of the 74 executions this year, only 10 percent were punishment for the murder of a Black person, yet Blacks are victims in about 50 percent of the murders committed in the U.S. Their deaths rarely merit the attention and the expenditures associated with the death penalty. Since the death penalty was reinstated, six White defendants have been executed for murdering a Black person, while 112 Black people have been executed for the murder of a White person.

Lack of competent representation continued to contribute to the arbitrariness of the death penalty. Exzavious Gibson, a poor Black man in Georgia, went before the Georgia courts to appeal his death sentence without a lawyer to plead his case. He lost the appeal. In Mississippi, a federal civil rights suit was filed on behalf of death row inmates against the state, which provides no money and no attorneys for the post-conviction appeals process. The suit cited the results of psychological testing given to the inmates, which showed that one-third suffered from mental retardation. The inmates also were given the Law School Admission Test to test the assumption that they could act as their own lawyers (none of the inmates scored above the 1 percent level)....

... In the past, representation in Georgia and Mississippi might have been provided by the death penalty resource centers, which were established to help with appeals. But federal funding for these centers in 20 states around the country was cut off in 1996, leaving many inmates unrepresented.

The increasing frequency of executions in the U.S. has done little to settle the issue in the eyes of the public. Opposition has moved from candlelight vigils outside of penitentiaries to national and international critiques of the continuing arbitrariness and inequity in the implementation of the death penalty. Public disillusionment with the political promises made for capital punishment is evidenced in the high support for alternatives to executions. While the trend toward more executions will likely continue because of the vast number of people on death row and the shorter appeals process, there are signs that the public may be shifting its focus away from the death penalty as a solution to crime.

STATEMENT OF REPRESENTATIVE HENRY B. GONZALEZ (D-TX) IN THE HOUSE OF REPRESENTATIVES, JUNE 30, 1995

... I believe that the death penalty is an act of vengeance veiled as an instrument of justice. Not only do I believe that there are independently sufficient moral objections to the principle of capital punishment to warrant its abolition, but I also know that the death penalty is meted out to the poor, to a disproportionate number of minorities, and does not either deter crime or advance justice.

Violent crimes have unfortunately become a constant in our society.... The sight of any brutal homicide excites a passion within us that demands retributive (exacting punishment for offense done) justice.... We cannot allow ourselves to punish an irrational action with an equally irrational retaliation — murder is wrong, whether it is committed by an individual or by the state.

... The United Nations Universal Declaration of Human Rights states, "No one shall be subjected to torture or to cruel, inhuman, or degrading treatment or punishment." The death penalty is torture, and numerous examples exist, emphasizing the cruelty of the execution....

... Studies fail to establish that the death penalty either has a unique value as a deterrent or is a more effective deterrent than life imprisonment. We assume that perpetrators will give greater consideration to the consequences of their actions if the penalty is death, but the problem is that we are not always dealing with rational actions. Those who commit violent crimes often do so in moments of passion, rage, and fear — times when irrationality reigns.

... Proponents advocate that some crimes simply deserve death. This argument is ludicrous. If a murderer deserves death, I ask why then do we not burn the arsonist or rape the rapist? Our justice system does not provide for such punishments because society comprehends that it must be founded on principles different from those it condemns. How can we condemn killing while condoning execution?

... In practice, capital punishment has become a kind of grotesque lottery. It is more likely to be carried out in some states than in others.... The death penalty is far more likely to be imposed against Blacks than Whites.... It is most likely to be imposed upon the poor and uneducated — 60 percent of death row inmates never finished high school....

... There are moves in Congress to speed up the execution process by limiting and streamlining the appeals process. But when the statistics show how arbitrarily the death penalty is applied, how can we make any changes without first assuring fairness?... There are no do-overs in this business when mistakes are made....

EXCERPTS FROM JUSTICE HARRY A. BLACKMUN'S DISSENTING OPINION IN THE SUPREME COURT DECISION *CALLINS V. JAMES* (510 U.S. 1141, 1994),

DENYING REVIEW OF THE DEATH PENALTY CASE (SEE JUSTICE SCALIA'S CONCURRING OPINION IN CHAPTER X)

... Twenty years have passed since this Court declared that the death penalty must be imposed fairly, and with reasonable consistency, or not at all, and, ... despite the effort of the states and courts to devise legal formulas and procedural rules to meet this daunting challenge, the death penalty remains fraught with arbitrariness, discrimination, caprice, and mistake.... Experience has taught us that the constitutional goal of eliminating arbitrariness and discrimination from the administration of death ... can never be achieved without compromising an equally essential component of fundamental fairness — individualized sentencing....

From this day forward, I no longer shall tinker with the machinery of death. For more than 20 years, I have endeavored — indeed, I have struggled — along with a majority of this Court, to develop procedural and substantive rules that would lend more than the mere appearance of fairness to the death penalty endeavor. Rather than continue to coddle the Court's delusions that the desired level of fairness has been achieved and the need for regulation eviscerated (removed), I feel morally and intellectually obligated simply to concede that the death penalty experiment has failed. It is virtually self-evident to me now that no combination of procedural rules or substantive regulations ever can save the death penalty from its inherent constitutional deficiencies.... The problem is that the inevitability of factual, legal, and moral error gives us a system that we know must wrongly kill some defendants, a system that fails to deliver the fair, consistent, and reliable sentence of death required by the Constitution....

There is little doubt now that *Furman's* essential holding was correct. (See Chapter II.) Although most of the public seems to desire, and the Constitution appears to permit, the penalty of death, it surely is beyond dispute that, if the death penalty cannot be administered consistently and rationally, it may not be administered at all.

Delivering on the *Furman* promise, however, has proved to be another matter. *Furman* aspired to eliminate the vestiges of racism and the effects of poverty in capital sentencing; it deplored the "wanton" and "random" infliction of death by a government with constitutionally limited power. *Furman* demanded that the sentencer's discretion be directed and limited by procedural rules and objective standards in order to minimize the risk of arbitrary and capricious sentences of death.

... It soon became apparent that discretion could not be eliminated from capital sentencing without threatening the fundamental fairness due a defendant when life is at stake. Just as contemporary society was no longer tolerant of the random or discriminatory infliction of the penalty of death, ... evolving standards of decency required due consideration of the uniqueness of each individual defendant when imposing society's ultimate penalty....

... While one might hope that providing the sentencer with as much relevant mitigating (lessening the gravity of crime) evidence as possible will lead to more rational and consistent sentences, experience has taught otherwise. It seems that the decision whether a human being should live or die is so inherently subjective — rife with all of life's understandings, experiences, prejudices, and passions — that it inevitably defies the rationality and consistency required by the Constitution....

STATEMENT OF SENATOR CAROL MOSELEY-BRAUN (D-CA) BEFORE THE SENATE JUDICIARY COMMITTEE, APRIL 1, 1993

... [T]he Supreme Court's recent holding in the *Herrera* case (see Chapter III), that a death row inmate's claim of actual innocence does not entitle him to *habeas* relief (a prisoner's petition to be heard in federal court), is deeply troubling in an era when Congress and state legislatures are rushing to make more and more crimes punishable by death yet simultaneously curtailing the right to appeal at both the state and federal levels....

When human judgment becomes infallible, our system will be infallible. Until then, those who would strip the system of vital safeguards lead us ever closer to the day when, in the name of the state, we will execute an innocent man. And that, in the word of Justice Brennan's dissent in the *Herrera* case, "comes perilously close to simple murder."

STATEMENT OF WALTER MCMILLIAN, MONROEVILLE, ALABAMA, BEFORE THE SENATE JUDICIARY COMMITTEE, APRIL 1, 1993

My name is Walter McMillian. I was sentenced to die in the electric chair and spent nearly six years on death row in Alabama awaiting execution for a murder that I did not commit, a murder that I knew nothing about, a murder that I had nothing to do with. Today, the state of Alabama has acknowledged that I am an innocent man and that I was wrongfully convicted. What happened to me could have happened to you, or to anyone else. I was convicted and sentenced to death on the false testimony of one man. I am here today to urge you to do all that is in your power to prevent what happened to me from happening to anyone else.

TESTIMONY OF JULIUS L. CHAMBERS, DIRECTOR-COUNSEL, NAACP LEGAL DEFENSE AND EDUCATIONAL FUND, INC., BEFORE THE HOUSE JUDICIARY COMMITTEE, MARCH 14, 1990

... [P]assage of the proposed death penalty bills would not advance — but would instead retard — resolution of the vexing problems associated with urban crime. While holding up the mirage of fighting and deterring crime, these death penalty bills would surely result in furthering the historical and well-documented racial disparities in the imposition of capital punishment in the United States.

Our concern is squarely grounded in the stark reality, which Black people have traditionally faced. For more than three centuries, the weight of the death penalty in this country has been borne far more heavily by Blacks than by Whites....

... There is no question that the financial cost of sentencing a single person to death is astronomical.... For example, the GAO (General Accounting Office) noted that one study done on "death penalty costs in New York estimated it would cost at least $1.8 million to defend and prosecute a capital case." By contrast, the cost of feeding and housing the defendant convicted in that same case for a period of 40 years would only be $602,000. The proposed statutes are absolutely silent as to where the millions of dollars would come from to "foot the bill...."

Perhaps the true purpose of the bills is to divert the public's attention away from considering measures which could truly serve to fight crime. One commentator correctly observed that ... "the death penalty debate enables public officials and legislators to falsely assert that they are being tough on crime because they favor the death penalty." More emphasis should be placed on the less glamorous side of fighting crime. Most major cities in the country, for example, cannot afford to offer adequate treatment to young offenders who have become ensnared with the drug world....

TESTIMONY OF HENRY SCHWARZ-CHILD, DIRECTOR, AMERICAN CIVIL LIBERTIES UNION (ACLU) CAPITAL PUNISHMENT PROJECT, BEFORE THE HOUSE JUDICIARY COMMITTEE, MARCH 14, 1990

The American Civil Liberties Union ... hold[s] capital punishment to be inherently cruel and unusual punishment, barred by the Eighth Amendment of the Constitution. We conclude, furthermore, that in its application, the death penalty violates the due-process-of-law clause of the Fifth Amendment and the equal-protection-of-the-law clause of the Fourteenth. These judgments are grounded in the evidence that the retention of the death penalty in no way contributes to a lessening of the incidence of violent crime, that executions are a barbaric spectacle inflicted upon isolated individual criminal offenders in circumstances redolent with arbitrariness, racial and sex discrimination, as well as status bigotry, that entirely innocent persons are unavoidably executed on occasion, and that the death penalty is not only staggeringly expensive to administer but radically distorts the entire scheme of criminal sentencing.

No one — I want to emphasize — opposes the death penalty because we think that violent crime is not so terrible or that punishment for it should not be proportionately severe. It is the *limits* of severity that is in controversy, not deep anguish about violent crime; that latter, we all, of course, share. When 200 years ago Western countries, including ours, abolished medieval forms of criminal punishment — drawing and quartering, boiling in oil, burning at the stake, gibbeting (hanging), and their like — we did so not because crimes were no longer thought to be so bad or because criminals had become nicer people: Those brutal forms of execution were abolished because we had come to think of *ourselves* as too civilized to do that sort of thing to another human being, no matter who he or she was or what [he or she] had done. *That*, and not the baseless claim that execution makes for less crime, is the issue....

REVEREND GUILLERMO CHAVEZ, CHAIRMAN, NATIONAL INTERRELIGIOUS TASK FORCE ON CRIMINAL JUSTICE, BEFORE THE HOUSE JUDICIARY COMMITTEE, NOVEMBER 7, 1985

... I question the notion of "standards of decency" as an accepted rationale upon which to base public policy. We need to remember that, about 200 years ago, slaveholding was not considered offensive to the then-current "standards of decency."

... As people of religious and ethical conscience, we seek the restoration and the renewal of wrongdoers, not their deaths. Capital punishment makes it possible for human error or preju-

dice to send innocent persons to their death. It eliminates forever the healing possibilities of human love and respect. Penal history provides us with prominent examples of innocent persons falsely condemned. Our Judeo-Christian heritage affirms that for the state to assume the power of absolute judgment is to assume a power that belongs only to God.

Another issue that concerns us is that the value of life, when confronted with the death penalty, is cheapened. In this regard, we are especially concerned with what the death penalty does to a society that inflicts it.

As the United Presbyterian Church has declared, "The use of the death penalty tends to brutalize the society that condones it." In denying the humanity of those we put to death, even those guilty of the most terrible crimes, including espionage or treason, we deny our own humanity, and life is further cheapened. Nothing is achieved by taking one more life or adding one more victim.

REMARKS OF SUPREME COURT JUSTICE THURGOOD MARSHALL AT A JUDICIAL CONFERENCE OF THE SECOND CIRCUIT IN HERSHEY, PENNSYLVANIA, SEPTEMBER 6, 1985

... [C]apital defendants frequently suffer the consequences of having trial counsel who are ill-equipped to handle capital cases. Death penalty litigation has become a specialized field of practice, and even the most well-intentioned attorneys often are unable to recognize, preserve, and defend their client's rights. Often trial counsel simply are unfamiliar with the special rules that apply in capital cases. Counsel — whether appointed or retained — often are handling their first criminal cases, or their first murder cases, when confronted with the prospect of a death penalty. Though acting in good faith, they inevitably make very serious mistakes.... The federal reports are filled with stories of counsel who presented *no* evidence in mitigation (lessening of the gravity of the crime) of their client's sentences because they did not know what to offer or how to offer it, or had not read the state's sentencing statute.

... The Court has not yet recognized that the right of effective assistance must encompass a right to counsel familiar with death penalty jurisprudence at the trial stage. Instead, in all but the most egregious (outstanding for undesirable qualities) case, a court cannot or will not make a finding of ineffective assistance of counsel, because counsel has met what the Supreme Court has defined as a minimal standard of competence for criminal lawyers. As a consequence, many capital defendants find that errors by their lawyers preclude presentation of substantial constitutional claims, but that such errors — with the resulting forfeitures of rights — are not sufficient in themselves to constitute ineffective assistance.

Contrary to popular perceptions, all capital defendants have *not* spent years filing frivolous claims in federal courts. Many of these defendants have not yet filed *any* federal claims when their execution dates are set. We simply cannot allow this inaccurate view to blind us to reality or to accept the hasty review process on the ground that defendants already have had the benefits of an untruncated (lengthy) review process. Until an execution date is set and the situation becomes urgent, capital defendants simply have been unable to secure counsel.

Once the execution date is set, the race is on. Prisoners who have not yet sought state or federal *habeas corpus* relief have roughly one month to do so.... But the new attorney often has no knowledge of the record, has not met the client, and has only a few days to read hundreds of pages of transcripts and prepare a petition. This petition, hastily prepared, must include all claims that the defendant might raise, because subsequent petitions will likely be declared abusive of the process if they entertain collateral attacks....

IMPORTANT NAMES AND ADDRESSES

American Bar Association
Criminal Justice Section
740 15th St. NW
Washington, DC 20005-1022
(202) 662-1500
FAX (202) 662-1032
www.abanet.org
abasvcctr@abanet.org

American Civil Liberties
Union
Capital Punishment Project
122 Maryland Ave. NE
Washington, DC 20002
(202) 544-1681
FAX (202) 546-0738
www.aclu.org
capitalpunishment@aclu.org

Amnesty International
U.S.A.
600 Pennsylvania Ave. SE
5th Floor
Washington, DC 20003
(202) 544-0200
FAX (202) 546-7142
www.amnestyusa.org
aiusama@aiusa.org
New York Office:
322 Eighth Ave.
New York, NY 10001
(212) 807-8400
FAX (212) 627-1451

Death Penalty Information
Center
1320 18th St. NW
5th Floor
Washington, DC 20036
(202) 293-6970
FAX (202) 822-4787
www.essential.org/dpic
dpic@essential.org

Federal Bureau of
Investigation
935 Pennsylvania Ave. NW
Washington, DC 20535
(202) 324-3000
FAX (202)324-1524
www.fbi.gov

Federal Bureau of Prisons
320 First St. NW
Washington, DC 20534
(202) 307-3198
FAX (202) 514-6878
www.bop.gov
webmaster@bop.gov

Innocence Project
Benjamin N. Cardozo
School of Law
55 Fifth Ave.
New York, NY 10003
(212) 790-0200
www.yu.edu/cardozo/law/
innocent.html

International Association
of Chiefs of Police
515 N. Washington St.
Alexandria, VA 22314
(703) 836-6767
FAX (703) 836-4543
www.theiacp.org
information@theiacp.org

Justice Research and
Statistics Association
777 N. Capital St. NE #801
Washington, DC 20002
(202) 842-9330
FAX (202) 842-9329
www.jrsainfo.org
cjinfo@jrsa.org

Murder Victims Families
for Reconciliation
2161 Massachusetts Ave.
Cambridge, MA 02140
(617) 868-0007
FAX (617) 354-2832
www.mvfr.org

NAACP Legal Defense
and Educational Fund, Inc.
99 Hudson St., Suite 1600
New York, NY 10013-2897
(212) 965-2200
FAX (212) 219-2052
www.ldfla.org/ldf

National Association of
Criminal Defense Lawyers
1025 Connecticut Ave. NW,
Suite 901
Washington, DC 20036
(202) 872-8600
FAX (202) 872-8690
www.nacdl.org
assist@nacdl.com

National Center for
Victims of Crime
2111 Wilson Blvd., #300
Arlington, VA 22201
(800) 394-2255
(703) 276-2880
FAX (703) 276-2889
www.ncvc.org
ncvc@ncvc.org

National District Attorneys
Association
99 Canal Center Plaza
Alexandria, VA 22314
(703) 549-9222
FAX (703) 836-3195
www.ndaa.org

National Institute of Justice
810 Seventh St. NW
Washington, DC 20531
(202) 307-2942
FAX (202) 307-6394
www.ojp.usdoj.gov/nij

The Sentencing Project
1516 P St. NW
Washington, DC 20005
(202) 628-0871
FAX (202) 628-1091
www.sentencingproject.org
staff@sentencingproject.org

U.S. Commission on Civil
Rights
624 9th St. NW
Washington, DC 20425
(202) 376-7533
Complaints: (800) 552-6843
FAX (202) 376-7597
www.usccr.gov

U.S. Department of Justice
950 Pennsylvania Ave. NW
Washington, DC 20530-0001
(202) 514-2007
FAX (202) 514-5331
www.usdoj.gov
web@usdoj.gov

U.S. Department of Justice
Bureau of Justice Statistics
810 Seventh St. NW
Washington, DC 20531
(202) 307-0765
(800) 732-3277
FAX (202) 307-5846
www.ojp.usdoj.gov/bjs
askbjs@ojp.usdoj.gov

U.S. House Judiciary
Committee
2138 Rayburn House
Office Bldg.
Washington, DC 20515
(202) 225-3951
FAX (202) 225-7682
www.house.gov/judiciary
judiciary@mail.house.gov

U.S. Senate Judiciary
Committee
Dirksen Senate Office Bldg.
Room SD-224
Washington, DC 20510
(202) 224-5225
FAX (202) 224-9102
www.senate.gov/~judiciary

U.S. Sentencing
Commission
1 Columbus Circle NE
Suite 2-500 South Lobby
Washington, DC 20002-8002
(202) 273-4500
FAX (202) 273-4529
www.ussc.gov
pubaffairs@ussc.gov

U.S. Supreme Court
1 First St. NE
Washington, DC 20543
(202) 479-3211

RESOURCES

The U.S. Department of Justice collects statistics on death row inmates as part of its "National Prisoner Statistics" (NPS) program. Based on voluntary reporting, the NPS program collects and interprets data on state and federal prisoners. Begun by the U.S. Bureau of the Census in 1926, the program was transferred to the Federal Bureau of Prisons in 1950, to the now-defunct Law Enforcement Assistance Administration (LEAA), and then to the Bureau of Justice Statistics (BJS) in 1979.

Since 1972, the Bureau of the Census, as the collecting agent for the LEAA and the BJS, has been responsible for compiling the relevant data. The BJS annually prepares a bulletin titled *Capital Punishment*, which provides an overview of capital punishment in the United States. The BJS *Sourcebook of Criminal Justice Statistics*, prepared by The Hindelang Criminal Justice Research Center of the State University at Albany, New York, is the most complete compilation of criminal justice statistics.

Postconviction DNA Testing: Recommendations for Handling Requests, a report by the National Commission on the Future of DNA Evidence of the National Institute of Justice (Washington, DC, 1999), was helpful in the preparation of this book. *Federal Death Penalty Cases: Recommendations Concerning the Cost and Quality of Defense Representation*, prepared by the Subcommittee on Death Penalty Cases of the Committee on Defender Services of the Judicial Conference of the United States (Washington, DC, 1998), provided information on the cost of federal death penalty cases.

The NAACP Legal Defense and Educational Fund, Inc. (LDF), is a private institution that maintains statistics on capital punishment. The LDF is strongly opposed to the death penalty. Despite its title, LDF is not part of the National Association for the Advancement of Colored People (NAACP),

although it was founded by that organization. For over 30 years, the New York-based LDF has had a separate board of directors, program, staff, office, and budget. The LDF publishes *Death Row, U.S.A.*, a periodic compilation of capital punishment statistics and information, including the names of all those currently on death row. Information Plus thanks the LDF for permission to use data from this semi-annual release.

Amnesty International is the Nobel Prize-winning human rights organization headquartered in London, England, United Kingdom. It strongly opposes the death penalty. Amnesty International maintains information on the death penalty and torture throughout the world and periodically publishes its findings. Information Plus would like to thank Amnesty International for permission to use its data on capital punishment around the world.

The Death Penalty Information Center (DPIC; Washington, DC), a non-profit organization, provides the media and general public with information and analysis regarding capital punishment. The DPIC, which is against the death penalty, serves as a resource to those working on this issue. Information Plus is grateful to the Death Penalty Information Center for permission to use its reports and charts on capital punishment.

The National Center for Victims of Crimes (Virginia), a non-profit organization that supports victims' rights and promotes victim assistance, was very helpful in providing information about the states that allow victims' families to witness executions.

Information Plus also thanks the Gallup Organization (New Jersey), Harris Interactive (New York), and the National Opinion Research Center of the University of Chicago (Illinois) for the use of their polls.

INDEX

Abolition/Abolitionist movement, 2-4, 5, *see also* Worldwide trend
Ake v. Oklahoma, 34-35, 52
American Convention on Human Rights, 48, 90
Amnesty International, 83ff
Anti-Drug Abuse Act, 4, 37, 48
Anti-Terrorism and Effective Death Penalty Act, 4, 5, 59, 68, 69
Arbitrariness/Capriciousness of the death penalty, 6-7, 18, 19, 40
Arizona v. Fulminante, 21-22
Baldus Study, 38-40, 70
Barefoot v. Estelle, 32-33
Batson v. Kentucky, 41
Beck v. Alabama, 11
Beets, Betty Lou, 55
Bifurcated (two-part) trial system, 8, 66
Booth v. Maryland, 27-28
Branch v. Texas, 6-7
Breard, Angel Francisco, 68, 85
Breard v. Netherland, 85
Bruton v. U.S., 22
Bryan v. Moore, 50
Buenoano, Judy, 54-55
Bush, Governor Jeb, 50
Bush, President George, 4
Cabana v. Bullock, 17
Caldwell v. Mississippi, 12
California First Amendment Society v. Calderon, 52
Callins v. James, 93-94, 104-105
Campbell v. Wood, 42
Chapman v. California, 21, 23
Clinton, First Lady Hillary Rodham, 68
Clinton, President William (Bill), 69
Coerced confession, 21-22
Coker v. Georgia, 15, 44, 58
Commutation, 5, 60, 61
Competency standard, 37
Constitutionality of the death penalty, 7-8, 58
  hanging, 42
  lethal gas, 43
Court cases, 6-43
Cruel and unusual punishment, 6-8, 9, 13, 19, 31, 35, 44, 47, 48, 49, 50, 52
Death row inmates, 59ff
  age, 62
  automatic review, 66-67

criminal history, 61, 64-65
  education, 62, 64
  federal, 60-61, 69
  foreign nationals, 85
  gender, 61
  Illinois, 71
  marital status, 64
  number, 59-60
  race and ethnicity, 61-62
  removal from death row, 65-66
  states, 61
  time on death row, 65
Deterrence, 2, 51
DNA evidence/testing, 69-70, 76
Douglass, Senator Brooks, 52
Eddings v. Oklahoma, 29, 30
Eighth Amendment, 6-7, 9, 13, 14, 16, 24-25, 28, 29, 31, 32, 42, 43, 44, 47, 48
Enmund v. Florida, 16-17
Estelle v. Smith, 34
Everheart v. Georgia, 15, 44
Evidence
  newly discovered, 24-26, 69
  suppressed, 26
Executions, *see also* Worldwide trend
  costs, 71-74
  crimes committed, 57-58
  federal, 4
  foreign nationals, 85
  gender, 54-56
  mentally retarded, 36-37, 48
  methods, 58
  military, 53
  minors, 30-32, 47-48, 90
  number, 53-54, 59
  postponement, 20-21, 68, 85
  public/private, 51
  race and ethnicity, 55, 57
  states, 54, 55
  witnesses to, 45, 51-52
Executive clemency, 25
Exonerations, 68, 69, 76
Fierro v. Gomez, 43
Fifth Amendment, 21, 34, 47
First Amendment, 42, 52
Ford v. Georgia, 40-41
Ford v. Wainwright, 35-36
Fourteenth Amendment, 6, 9, 10, 13, 16, 20, 21, 23, 25, 35, 41, 43
Furman v. Georgia, 5, 6-7, 8, 44
Gilmore, Gary, 6, 49
Godfrey v. Georgia, 18

Godinez v. Moran, 37
Gomez v. Fierro, 43
Gregg v. Georgia, 7-8, 16
Habeas corpus petition, 4, 5, 20-21, 68, 69, 85
Harmless-error standard, 21-23
Harris v. Alabama, 14
Heckler v. Chaney, 41-42, 51
Herrera v. Collins, 24-26, 69-70
History, 2-4
Hitchcock v. Dugger, 16
Hynes v. Tomei, 47
Innocence, 24-26, 27, 68-70
Innocence Protection Act of 2000, 69
Insanity, 34-36
International Covenant on Civil and Political Rights, 48, 81, 90
Jackson v. Georgia, 6-7
Johnson v. Texas, 31-32
Judge sentencing, 13-14, 23
Jurek v. Texas, 7-9, 33
Jury as advisory panel, 13-14
Jury selection, 73
  cross-section of community, 10
  exclusion from capital case similar to exclusion from noncapital case, 10
  exclusion of death penalty opponents, 9-10
Kentucky Racial Justice Act, 45, 71
Kidnapping, 15, 44
Kyles v. Whitley, 26
Lankford v. Idaho, 23-24
Laws, 44 ff
  challenges, 46-47
  changes, 44
  federal, 4, 45, 46
  mental retardation, 48
  methods of execution, 48-51
  military, 4
  minimum age for execution, 47-48
  Native Americans, 4
  states, 44-45
Lockett v. Ohio, 9, 15-16, 29
Lockhart v. McCree, 10
Louisiana v. Wilson, 46-47
McCleskey v. Kemp, 38-40, 70
McFarland v. Scott, 20-21
McVeigh, Timothy J., 4, 51, 78
Mease, Darrell, 5
Minors, *see also* Executions
  tried as adults, 48
Miranda v. Arizona, 34

INDEX (Continued)

Miscarriage of justice, claim of, 26
Moratorium, 5, 53, 68-69, 75
  de facto, 5, 6
Murray v. Carrier, 26
Murray v. Giarratano, 20
Paraguay et al. v. Gilmore, 85
Payne v. Tennessee, 27-28
Pennsylvania v. Finley, 20
Penry v. Lynaugh, 32, 36-37
Peremptory challenges, 40-41
Pope John Paul II, 5, 100
Porter, Anthony, 68
Proffitt v. Florida, 7-8
Provenzano v. Moore, 49
Psychiatric testimony, 32-37
Public attitudes, 75-80
  deterrent, 89
  for murder, 76
  frequency of imposition, 78-79
  innocence, 79-80
  life without parole, 76-77
  specific crimes, 77-78
  support, 75-76
  types of crime, 80
Public defender system, 67-68
Pulley v. Harris, 19
Racial prejudice, 37-41, 69, 70-71, 85
Rape, 2, 15, 44, 45, 46-47, 58
  Louisiana, 44, 46-47, 58
  Mississippi, 45
Relin v. Mateo, 47
Right to counsel, 19-20, 71-72
Roberts v. Louisiana, 8, 9
Rudolph v. Alabama, 5

Rush, Benjamin, 2-3
Ryan, Governor George H., 69
Sawyer v. Whitley, 26
Schlup v. Delo, 26
Sellers, Sean, 48
Sentencing criteria
  absence at scene of crime, 16
  aggravating circumstances, 8, 13, 14, 23-24, 46
  characteristics of criminal, 8, 14, 15-16, 27, 46
  circumstances of crime, 8, 15-16, 27, 46
  comparative proportionality review, 18-19
  consideration of lesser charge, 9, 11
  future threat to society, 8-9, 12-13, 32-33, 34
  intent, 16-17, 18, 22-23, 27, 31-32
  malice, 22-23
  mitigating factors, 8, 9, 13, 14, 15-16, 27-28
    mental retardation, 48
    youth, 29-32
  outrageous murder, 18
  possibility of parole, 12, 32
  victim impact statements, 27-28, 46
Simmons v. South Carolina, 12-13
Sixth Amendment, 10, 13, 20, 40-41, 47
Society for the Abolition of Capital Punishment, 3
South Carolina v. Gathers, 28
Spaziano v. Florida, 13, 14

Stanford v. Kentucky, 30-31, 48
State v. Torrence, 67
Swain v. Alabama, 40, 41
Thompson v. Oklahoma, 30
Tison v. Arizona, 17-18
Treason, 2, 15, 44,
Trifurcated (three-part) trial system, 13
Tucker, Karla Faye, 54
Turner v. Murray, 37-38
United Nations Convention on the Rights of the Child, 48, 90
United Nations resolutions/initiatives, 81, 82
United States v. Jackson, 47
Vienna Convention on Consular Relations, 85
Viewpoints, abolition of capital punishment
  con, 91-99
  pro, 100-108
Violent Crime Control and Law Enforcement Act (Federal Death Penalty Act of 1994), 4, 49, 72
Wainwright v. Witt, 9-10
Wilkins v. Missouri, 30-31, 48
Witherspoon v. Illinois, 9, 10, 11
Woodson v. North Carolina, 8, 9
Worldwide trend, 5, 81-90
  abolitionist countries, 83, 88
  de facto abolitionist countries, 88
  retentionist countries, 83-85
Yates v. Evatt, 23